TEARS OF HOPE

Dear Linda,

I am so blessed to have you as a Global woman peace network sister.

With love and light

2019

NOTE: In order to make *Tears of Hope* easy to read for people of all ages, backgrounds, and non-native English speakers, an effort was made to write it in a light, informal style using everyday language.

Tears of Hope

Aimmee Kodachian

Published by Motivational Press, Inc.
2360 Corporate Circle
Suite 400
Henderson, NV 89074
www.MotivationalPress.com

www.EmpoweringSoulsINT.com

To protect certain identities, some names have been changed.

Manufactured in the United States of America.

ISBN: 978-1-62865-020-4

Contents

LETTER FROM AIMMEE

Everyone has a story to tell. In this book, I have the privilege to share mine. When I sit back and look at my life today, I'm amazed at how much it has changed. Despite being such a private person, I felt compelled to share my story to help others Rise Above and See Light Through Darkness.

When I wrote this book, I thought it would give me the opportunity to help women. Now I realize that it reaches everyone; women, men and even teenagers.

During the early stages of sharing the manuscript, I received many responses from people of all ages and backgrounds telling me how my story had touched their lives. Their comments gave me inexplicable happiness and confirmed that every experience I've gone through in my life happened for a reason.

Yet this book is not just about me. I am one of the millions of people worldwide who have experienced war and tragedies. This story is about overcoming adversities by keeping your faith and hope alive.

While recording the events of my life on paper, I learned more about myself and that nothing is impossible as long as you maintain the will to do it. I believe that God guided me through this process of sharing my story with you.

It is my desire that when you read Tears of Hope, it will help you to see your life in a different perspective and touch you in a special way.

With Love and Light,
Aimmee Kodachian

ACKNOWLEDGEMENTS

Tom, my husband and soulmate. You believed in me and stood behind me during the good and bad. You constantly give me your all and have allowed me to live my purpose. From the bottom of my heart, I love you.

My father Pierre. You loved me deeply and helped me see life in a different perspective.

My mom Antoinette. Thank you for giving me life and for loving me.

My brothers Jacque, Robert, Elie and my sister Jacqueline. Each one of you has a special place in my heart.

My brother-in-law Salim and my sisters-in-law Aghavnie and Joceline. Thank you for welcoming me into your hearts!

My precious daughter Silva. My love for you helped me to keep going every day. I love you so much and I'm so proud of you!

My grandchildren Steven, Sovante, Kasandra, and Izel. It is a blessing to have you in my life!

My brother Roger. I have a special connection with you. We shared and lived many painful memories together. You are a hero in my eyes and I am so proud to call you brother.

Nouhad Raphael, Maral Kabranian, Rosin Deovletian, Lelia Herfurth, Ghada Assaf and Rebecca Kodachian. You have witnessed many chapters of my life. Thank you for being there for me!

Eden Stenger, LaNette Solmes, Machala Danieri, Stacie Weaver, Attorney Rod Buttars, Judi Moreo, Patricia Fripp, Darren LaCroix, Keith Keller, Liz Nitta, Darlene Mea, Danielle J Duperret, Paul and Melodie Williams, Vicki Kallman, Cheri Hickman, Regina Murphy, Jordana Carroll, Narayanan Doraswamy, Cheryl L Baker, Josh Carpenter, Charmaine Lee, Eliane Ayele Amavigan, Michael Franklin, Marquetta Goodwin, Maria Boyd, Janice Greever, Diana Lamadrid, Don Saunders, Ephraim Armendariz, Katia Cheetany, Jaclynn Pham. Each of you have believed and supported me in your own unique way. Thank you!

Stephanie Thompson. Your belief in me means the world. Thank you for helping me deliver my message through your incredible voice. Because of you, the Rise Above song will touch countless people's lives.

Wendy Y. Tucker. Thank you for helping me to reconstruct years of my life on paper. You were such an important part of writing the original Tears of Hope.

Eric Johnson. Thank you for editing my writing, helping with grammar, and giving me the opportunity to take Tears of Hope to the next level. You can reach Eric at wordswitheric@gmail.com.

My publisher Justin Sachs. Your belief in this project will allow countless people to experience Tears of Hope. Thank you for your support and believing in my message.

I am so grateful for all of you. Thank you!

*This book is dedicated to everyone who
wants to Rise Above and help
the world be a better place.*

CHAPTER ONE

An Unforgettable Day

D o you believe there is a reason for everything? I strongly believe that there is a *reason you* picked up this book and started to read it. I encourage you to open your heart and mind and look for the *hidden* messages that may be waiting for *you*!

I was twelve years old when my father broke the news that our home country of Lebanon was facing difficulties and on the brink of war. With a concerned face, he shared his plan, "I want to keep all of you safe, so we are going to move to Egypt."

Two weeks later, he called our family into the living room for a meeting. "The country's situation is growing worse," dad said. We sat there, closely listening as he continued, "We all need to wrap things up soon and leave before the war breaks out."

For the first time in a long time, I sat there watching and enjoying that my family was listening to each other with harmony and love, which was rare.

After the family meeting was over, my parents went into the next room to listen to the radio, anxious to hear updates about the state of our country. My siblings left the house, and my older and favorite brother Robert and I stayed in the living room.

It was a beautiful day with a soft breeze. The sky was clear blue. I was relaxing and enjoying the day, still wearing my new long nightdress, which was bright white with soft pink flowers. It reminded me of a beautiful and peaceful spring field.

Robert and I were having a great conversation. We realized that it was noon when we heard the familiar news theme music playing on the radio.

"I can't believe it is noon already," he said. The morning had flown by.

"Me neither," I said. We both smiled and continued talking.

A few moments later, my father yelled, "Robert, don't go anywhere today. The news is not good."

"Don't worry. I won't." Robert responded. "I'm going to spend time with Aimmee today."

At that time, Robert was twenty years old. He was tall and handsome with thick wavy hair and beautiful dark eyes. Best of all, he had a big heart filled with love and light!

"What do you want to be when you grow up, Aimmee?" he asked.

This question took me off guard. No one had ever asked me what I wanted to be before. Just hearing that question and the sound of his soothing voice filled my heart with joy and excitement.

A smile formed on my face as I looked at Robert. I sat back in my wooden chair and told him without blinking, "I either want to be a lawyer because I want to help people who are treated unfairly or I want to be a teacher."

He asked, "Why do you want to be a teacher?"

"Well, everyone makes fun of me at school because I have difficulty reading. I'm not able to finish my homework. I can't even graduate from my class. They call me a loser but I know that I'm not one. I believe that everyone is different and special in their own way. The way I feel, regardless of our weaknesses or strengths, we all deserve to shine and feel good about ourselves. I want to be the kind of teacher that helps others to shine," I said with growing confidence.

This was the first time that I felt I could express my passions to someone who actually listened to me.

In that precious moment with my big brother, I realized that there was hope of my dreams coming true.

Seeing and hearing my excitement brought a smile to Robert's face. He continued, "I can understand why you would want to become a teacher. In order to live your dream, you must have a purpose or what I would call, a "WHY" that guides you. You definitely have that. I see that you *feel* it in your heart too. Now all you have to do is **believe** it in your mind. If you keep going in that direction Aimmee, nothing can stop you."

The power of his insightful words caused me to pause for a second.

I took a deep breath and looked at him with disappointment, and said, "Robert, yes it's true that I have my "why" and I feel it in my heart and soul. But I don't believe it. The reality is that I can't even graduate from my class. I could never reach the level of education needed to become a teacher! It is almost impossible for me to live my dream and become the teacher that I want to be."

With his attractive eyes and an encouraging look, he said, "I promise that I will help you with any difficulties you're having in school. There is no reason to worry. I'm here for you. You may not believe in yourself, but I believe in you!"

He disregarded my doubts about myself and continued asking about my future plans. I felt my spirit rise when he talked to me about going to college and eventually becoming a teacher. Just imagine, a Middle Eastern girl who never was able to graduate from her class now has hope that she can reach a much higher level of education. It felt like a dream!

I had discovered that you can achieve what you want no matter what. That was my first "aha" moment as a child, yet I knew that I needed more. I needed help and support from someone like Robert. Someone who believed in me and would help me make it happen.

I stood up and headed for the kitchen. "I'll get your tea, Robert," I said with the same smile still on my face. "Then we can pick up where we left off. I'll be right back.".

At that moment, Robert knew that I didn't want him to leave the room. It was obvious to him that I was having a wonderful time talking with him. He glanced at me with that gorgeous smile on his face as I went to get his black tea. I felt butterflies in my stomach. I was enthusiastically telling myself, "Yes! Yes! Yes!" and shaking my hands up and down with happiness. It was a beautiful moment and I was elated and full of hope.

I had only taken a couple of steps walking through the hallway toward the kitchen when not a second later, I heard a strange roaring sound followed by a loud whistle. Before I could blink an eye, our whole apartment shook with a loud crash. A bomb had come through the living room window. The bright moment that I was enjoying just seconds before suddenly vanished into darkness. The rooms became filled with thick haze and smoke. I started coughing, gasping for air. I could barely breathe. Everything became a blur. My eyes began to burn. My brand new white nightdress was now covered with black marks. Lebanon was no longer on the brink of war. Suddenly, war was a reality.

I quickly turned around. From the top of my lungs, I screamed out, "Robert! Robert!" All I saw was his hand. I couldn't see the rest of him. The entire room was in flames. Pieces of metal and wood, that surely would have killed me if I had not left the room a moment earlier, were sticking out of the wall as if they had been there all the time.

I couldn't believe this was happening. It felt like a different world. As a twelve year old, I was so confused. I kept wondering, "What is happening? Please, God, don't let anything happen to Robert." It was a nightmare that felt like it would never end.

My mother and father had been in the next room listening to the radio. When the bomb went off, my mother began to panic and started screaming. Disoriented and scared, I looked at my mom. I could see her holding onto the windowsill, trying to climb up and jump out. She thought she was running for safety, but in reality had no idea what she was doing. My father, who had maintained his composure, was forcefully holding her back. Yet she was fighting him with all her strength, trying to throw herself out the window. This incident occurred several times as she persistently kept trying to get out and dad would pull her safely back. Mom was frightened and out of control.

Standing there with fear and uncertainty, my eyes briefly met my father's. Within that moment, we exchanged looks of hopelessness. He wanted to reach out to me, his little girl who was standing helpless in the midst of the chaos. I imagine he was also thinking about Robert while he was preventing my mother from hurting herself.

The apartment continued to fill with smoke. All I could do was stand there as my world was spinning. Explosions and screaming filled my ears. Looking to the right, I saw the room where Robert was covered in flames. To my left, I saw my mother trying to jump out the window.

It was surreal. With every heartbeat, I denied the reality that was unfolding in front of my eyes. Life paused and everything was a blur.

One after another, the bombs kept striking the building. With each one, I was shaken to the core. As soon as I recovered my balance from one bomb, another would strike. Suddenly, my brother Elie and two other men broke through the front door. They helped my dad bring my mom down and away from the window. Then they hurriedly carried us both out of the apartment building. Elie firmly clutched onto my shaking body as he carried me out of the smoldering building. "Don't leave Robert!" I screamed as he held me. "You have to help Robert, Elie! Put me down. Go help Robert!"

Smoke gushed from the windows, especially from the living room where Robert and I had been talking only moments before. Behind us followed my father and the two other men moving my mother as fast as they could. With each step Elie took toward getting us to safety, I felt my body being rescued, while my heart was left behind in the flames. Left with Robert. My favorite brother. My hero. The one who believed in me and filled me with hope. With every painful breath I took, the agony inside of me grew. Robert was gone forever.

To make matters worse, I was tortured by this thought. "It should have been me who died, not Robert." Originally, I was going to stay in the living room and Robert was going to get his own tea. My mind was filled with endless questions. I asked God, "Why didn't you just take me too?"

All of my hopes and dreams were crushed. Robert had been taken from me right before my eyes. He was a passionate young man with great potential who had wanted to be an architect. If he had only lived longer, he could have accomplished incredible things. Lebanon had been on the brink of war, and Robert had just begun living his life. The war and its horrors started and my brother's life ended.

A few days after all the chaos, my father noticed that I was still scared and confused. He came over to me and put both of his arms on my shoulders. He bent down on his knee and gave me a big hug. "Aimmee", he said, "Don't be scared. I am here and everything is going to be all right." I cried on his shoulder, saying "I'm afraid, daddy". Then he gently pulled me away from him and said, "Aimmee, look at me. I want you to look straight into my eyes."

With love and compassion he continued, "our eyes have three parts," he said. "One white, one with color and one black. Do you see what I'm talking about?"

"Yes, I do," I answered. I still wasn't sure why he was telling me this. "You see the tiny black part of the eye, the innermost circle is called the pupil. We only see through the black part of our eye," he said. "Sometimes we have to go through darkness to see the *light*."

This was the unforgettable lesson that stayed in my mind and changed my perspective on life forever.

*   *   *

I was a twelve year old girl dealing with undiagnosed dyslexia. A so called "loser" who only made it to fourth grade. A girl who had lost hope in the dream of becoming a teacher. A child who was facing the realities of war and who continued to endure more of life's hardships filled with powerful lessons.

Just like my father shared his wisdom with me, I feel it's my turn to share my knowledge with you. I invite you into my life's journey and the lessons I learned that can help you see your life in a different perspective. My hope is that you will walk away Inspired, Empowered and Encouraged to take action towards a better life and begin seeing the *light* through darkness . . .

CHAPTER TWO

Growing up

Have you ever felt that your family is unique and different? Well I did. Let me introduce you to mine.

My father Pierre was an Armenian refugee. Along with many other Armenians during the 1940s, my father and his family moved to Lebanon. Thankfully, the Armenian people were welcomed in Lebanon.

Dad was creative and incredibly intelligent. In spite of only two years of formal schooling, he spoke five languages. He enjoyed expanding his knowledge about various subjects and spent hours reading and learning. Dad could carry on a stimulating conversation with anybody about any topic. To me, he seemed to know everything and it was all because of his passion for self-observation, education and discovery. In fact, people often called him a genius.

My mother Antoinette was a pretty Lebanese lady. She had a wonderful eye for color and a great sense of style. Along with being tall and in good shape, every time she went out she looked elegant. Hair fixed, nails done, each detail perfectly in place. To see her and how she dressed, you would have thought she was well-educated and from a well off family.

As a child, she loved school and playing with her classmates, but that didn't last long. It was difficult growing up while her father was dealing with his problem with alcohol. Since he continually kept giving in to his battle, my grandma Esma had to take over the family's financial burdens. Consequently, at a young age my mom was pressured to care for her younger siblings and forced to quit school. She never learned to read or write, and didn't get the chance to live a normal childhood.

My mother's memories of her father were painful. When he drank, he became violent. One day in a fit of rage, he took mom and one of my uncles out into the woods. If an innocent passerby hadn't stopped him, he surely would have killed them both. His behavior caused her to hate most men, while her *unhealthy* belief system affected the whole family at a great cost.

Around the age of twenty-five, my dad met my mother and they fell in love. They soon married. By that point, my mother had grown to enjoy the finer things in life. Although she didn't come from a rich family, she was born to live the lifestyle of the rich and famous. Her main focus was looking good in front of people. She always dressed to impress and was constantly hungry for attention. Unlike my father, my mom was not passionate about personal growth and simply lived in her own little world.

My mother's lack of common sense and awareness almost caused a tragedy in our family. One Sunday, when I was eight months old, my parents had a family gathering. As was the custom of most Lebanese families, they got together to have a feast, chat, drink and party all day long. After one of my family's barbecue gatherings, mom put me to bed and then put the still-smoldering barbecue grill in the same room as me. Since the windows were closed, the room filled with smoke and carbon monoxide. When my father came to check on me, I was turning blue and gasping for breath. He quickly rushed me outside into the fresh air and resuscitated me. Mom meant well. Harming me was not her intention. This was one of several times my life was saved.

The first two children of the family were Jacque and Jacqueline. Jacque, the first-born child, was fourteen years older than me. He was a child prodigy who conducted musical orchestras by the age of ten. Affectionately nicknamed the "Magic Child" by those who knew him,

Jacque was given the opportunity to perform in Armenia at a very young age. For three years, he lived and performed there.

My sister Jacqueline was born twelve years before me. She was the only girl out of four kids until my birth. As such, she was used to getting her own way and got whatever she wanted.

I already introduced you to my favorite childhood hero Robert. Even today when I think of him, my heart warms. Although he was eight years older than me, we really connected. He always treated me with love and respect. He was kind-hearted and very close to our family.

Years before I was born, my father was a sought-after cosmetologist who often won hairstyling contests in France. He owned several salons that employed over forty people and catered to socialites and celebrities. Dad was making quite a respectful living then, so he and mom were living the high life. They frequently attended parties where they socialized with rich and powerful people.

Dad was fairly popular. People either knew him from his salons, his inventions, or the articles he would occasionally write for the Armenian newspaper. Dad became a 33rd degree Grand Master freemason, the highest level. For a while, he even ran his own lodge.

During those more affluent times, Jacque and Jacqueline had a nanny. Mom had a housekeeper to take care of detailing the household, which she loved. Dad even had a personal chauffeur. My parents lived it up. Life was good . . . at least then.

My brother Elie's birth came during this affluent time of my family, six years before me. He was the fourth child and his dark features made him very handsome. As a kid, he had an aggressive personality. Just like me, he also struggled with a learning disability.

Financial success wasn't enough for my father. He needed to do what would satisfy his soul. One day, soon after Elie was born, he took mom out. They went to a boardwalk along the Mediterranean Sea called Raouche. In that beautiful place, dad told my mother about his desire to become an inventor. My mom's response was ugly.

In the months to come, when dad finally sold his thriving business in pursuit of his passion, mom became terribly upset. My father's decision dramatically changed the cushy and comfortable lifestyle to which she had become accustomed. She adamantly opposed his wish to change careers, yet he felt compelled to do it and from that point on, the family's foundation began to crumble. My parents started leading separate lives and grew further and further apart. We frequently heard this story retold by Mom who never forgot that day on the boardwalk.

My birth as the fifth child came in the winter of 1962 in Beirut, Lebanon in the midst of family turmoil. During that period, my parents were separated. After half a year of separation, fortunately, my father returned home. I was six months old before he saw me for the first time. Dad knew mom was very naive and couldn't survive without him. Like any good father, he missed his children and wanted to be with us.

By this time, our house featured a wide range of ages. Jacque was fifteen and Jacqueline was thirteen. Robert was eight, Elie was six and I was the new addition. Even a great mother would struggle raising five kids alone, and this further compelled my father to return home.

As a baby I was easy to take care of, so I was told. As a child, I was happy and fairly quiet. I had perfectionistic tendencies and was keenly aware of small details. If something was wrong, I felt a strong desire to fix it. If I saw a rock on a sidewalk, I'd want to move it so nobody would trip over it and get hurt. It was the protector side of me coming out. I felt a need to have things correct, right and organized, in order to prevent bad things from happening.

Having those characteristics made me vulnerable, especially at school when kids were treating me unfairly. My smile and happiness were taken away every time I was faced with bullying. In class, I was made fun of and picked on. It was constantly humiliating. I couldn't see letters on a page correctly and so I could not keep up academically with the other children. I eventually convinced mom to take me to the eye doctor.

When he told us that nothing was wrong with my eyes, my mother looked at me and said, "I can't believe this. You just wasted my time with your excuse." She pushed me, motioning me along as she said, "Let's go! Next time don't complain about something that's not there." I was dealing with a reading disability and yet the eye doctor wasn't looking for the source of the problem. Mom's reaction caused me to retreat into my shell and shut down. I started feeling as if people would never believe what I said. Not speaking up for myself caused me to suffer for many years. Mom's unhealthy beliefs affected her life in negative ways and now the same thing was beginning to happen to me. It is amazing how the smallest moments can affect your life.

My older sister Jacqueline was exceptionally intelligent at school. My mother would constantly compare me to her, asking, "Why can't you be more like your sister?" I sat there feeling confused.

I replied, "I'm trying as hard as I can but I can't do it." I couldn't compete with other students, let alone, my sister in terms of book knowledge. Deep inside, I would think *I wish someone could really get to know me. I don't like the feeling of being compared to others.*

Regardless of school and my reading disability, I was surprisingly a forward-thinking and insightful child.

It's true that I couldn't focus on a simple thing such as reading a page, but I was able to focus on life. I became very skilled at seeing and reading the real life stories all around me. It came naturally. I felt like I recognized and saw things that many people couldn't see, but I wasn't able to express what I felt. *How could I?*

Most adults judged me by my school grades. Giving my opinion about anything was not an option. They thought I wasn't smart enough. Although in my heart I knew that I was gifted, judgment from others drowned out and *stole* my happiness, uniqueness and identity.

Everyone has hidden gifts, strengths and weaknesses. Unfortunately, outside influences, people's words, and even our own internal fears can silence this power that *each* of us has.

It took me *decades* to regain my identity and voice. When I started to appreciate my gifts and uniqueness, I clearly understood that I don't have to be perfect to be beautiful and powerful. All I have to do is be myself.

*   *   *

Many times, our house was like a wrestling arena. Robert and Elie were good friends since they were so close in age, but like most brothers they fought a lot. It was always very loud with their roughhousing and fighting. Even though they fought, it was evident that they loved each other.

Despite my parents' rocky relationship, dad was always trying to appease mom. She preferred working over being a "stay at home" mother. In an attempt to make her happy, dad helped her open a nail salon close to home. Mom loved that business for its social outlet. Even though it took her mind off the pressures of home, at the end of the day she was always exhausted.

When I was five, there were two huge events. We celebrated my sister Jacqueline's wedding and my mother became pregnant. My parents were in their forties when my mother was with child for the last time. Another surprise quickly followed, my newlywed sister soon became pregnant too. Mom was not only having another baby, but also becoming a grandmother. With the regular craziness and my mother's hormones, life was always interesting! Between her pregnancy, running the salon and her teenage sons fighting, mom was constantly tired. She and everyone else were so busy that I was rarely noticed. Mom's focus became survival. She couldn't handle the pressure and was not able to be there completely for her children.

When my baby brother Roger was born, I felt like the happiest six year old in the world! Roger was new and exciting. He was a big, beautiful baby. Every time I had a chance, I would sneak onto the balcony without mom's knowledge and show him off to the neighborhood children passing by. Roger was like a doll to me. I loved him so much.

Dad would often take me to visit his mother, my Grandma Iskouhie. "Aimmee, you are so much like her," dad would say. This was the one comparison I loved. Grandma was wise, loving and caring. She was the one strong female figure in my life and I was so grateful. I knew that when I grew up, I wanted to be like her.

When she passed away, it was hard. I was still very young and wished I had been given the chance to get to know her better. It was also difficult for me to see my father depressed and heartbroken. That was my first experience losing a loved one. When I think of her now, I realize that I inherited her strong family values. Even today, her influence is evident in my life.

Over the years, the jagged rift between my parents had worsened. Regardless of their problems, there was no real option for divorce. In those days in Lebanon, divorce was almost unheard of. Even if it had been an option, my faithful father would never have left my mother. Each assumed that the other one would take care of us, but neither of them stepped up and actually took action. Both of them were already drained from their long, unhappy relationship. By the time Roger was a year old, my parents were sleeping in different rooms.

Even though they fought a lot, my parents were good, kind people. They loved us and each other. I believe that they were terribly mismatched in almost every way. It seemed the only things my parents had in common were their children and their love for the beach and parties. Since mom and dad were from different cultures and spoke different native languages, we were all given neutral French names. Sadly, our names were the only thing my parents ever compromised on.

Since my mother was emotionally and physically exhausted, I had to compensate for her lack of energy. At the early age of six, I began acting like Roger's mom. You can just imagine a little girl trying to fulfill the role of a mother! It was hard, but his love for me fueled my passion to always take care of him. As Roger grew older, just like Robert, he made me feel loved. His affection meant the world to me.

Dad was often traveling around this time. Every couple of months or so, he would leave for Syria, Egypt, or wherever else to sell his products. With his curious nature, dad created over one hundred different inventions. At first, these included cosmetics such as facial masks, hair growth products, and nail strengtheners. Eventually, he advanced to more complicated projects, including air fresheners and air purifiers. More than money, he dreamed of leaving a legacy behind by inventing something that would change the world. I was so close to my father that when he was gone, I felt alone and sad. Every time he left, I felt my heart grow heavy.

My father hoped to make adequate money so he could take better care of us. We always felt we were important to him, but he wasn't home enough. He didn't actually know what was going on in his own household. I wish he would have been more involved. Even though he was exceptionally intelligent, he still didn't realize that mom wasn't able to handle the responsibility of raising kids. He always gave her the benefit of the doubt. I don't know why.

Mom hated it when dad turned the kitchen into a working laboratory, filling the house with smoke and fumes. Seeing his equipment all over the place was a constant visual reminder of the lifestyle she had lost.

"Why do you have to clutter up the whole kitchen?" she would snap at him, rolling her eyes in disapproval as usual.

"Antoinette, you hardly cook. What's the big deal? I'm almost finished and I think this one's going to be successful," he would reply.

Dad did make money from his inventions, but he invested all of it into more of his ideas. Inventing became an addiction for him and brought financial problems to the family. This obsession was further destroying their relationship. Although I usually disagreed with my mother, I felt she had the right to be upset about this situation.

* * *

When dad would have an occasional social drink, mom's traumatic memories of her father would come back to haunt her. Her anger was based on projecting the memories of her father onto her husband. Those memories distorted her judgment. Drinking socially and abusing alcohol seemed to be the same thing in her mind. She did not understand the separation that exists with certain aspects of life. This showed me the power of looking at things from a different perspective. If mom had *recognized* and changed her negative association with alcohol, there would have been more peace in the house. When we step back from the situation and take a different viewpoint, it creates a new *awareness*. This results in peace and love, both in us and those around us.

Although dad's drinking never got out of control, another argument would ensue and she would badger him about his drinking. All of this was because of her memories of her father and her inability to recognize the source of her emotions.

"You act so stupid when you drink Pierre!" she yelled one evening.

"Antoinette, let's step outside," he said quietly. "You're going to wake the children."

Despite his efforts to calm things down, everyone including the neighbors could hear them.

"I don't want to go outside!" she yelled as he calmly took her by the arm, escorting her to the balcony.

Their constant arguing back and forth kept us kids awake most of the night. As I tried to drown out the noise by pulling the covers over my head, I prayed to God and asked him to stop their fighting. Little did I know that their problems would be small compared to the challenges ahead that were filled with life long lessons . . .

CHAPTER THREE

Beginning of the War

L et me take you back to 1975 again with more details, when my father broke the news to our family about the Lebanese Civil War. Dad wanted us to move to Egypt so we could be safe. Since he was traveling back and forth for business deals anyway, the timing was right and everything would work out.

I will never forget the day when we went to have our pictures taken for the passports. Traveling was new to me and sounded exciting. I was happily looking forward to the new adventure. I thought my dad wouldn't have to go on business trips anymore. Having him with us would mean the world to me.

We were the happiest we had been in a long time. Several months before the news of the impending war, Dad's inventions were just starting to payoff. He had found an investor to back the production of two of his numerous inventions. One was called Lavotex. It was an industrial strength solution to clean your hands without water. The second one was a special facial mask for rejuvenating skin.

By then, my brother Jacque had followed in my father's earlier footsteps and owned a hair salon. Both businesses were on the brink of becoming profitable and our financial situation was slowly improving. I enjoyed occasionally helping out in Jacque's salon. I would wait on the customers and get them coffee or whatever else they needed. It made me feel useful and grown up.

After dad had heard about the upcoming battle, he decided that he'd sell his share of the factory back to his investor and Jacque would sell his salon. That money would help us to start over in Egypt, our new home. Dad's inventions would be well received. He would take Lavotex and the mask there to open another factory. Mom would have her old lifestyle back and that would bring the family closer together.

A week after we took our passport pictures, we were all lounging around the house talking about the war and how different groups of people were starting to band together to protect each other. Then Robert made a most unusual statement, "I don't think I could handle seeing anyone hurt any of my family members."

Mom told him, "Don't worry, we are protected. God loves us."

"I don't believe in God," he replied.

"Yes, you do, Robert," Mom and I told him.

"No, I don't. If there is a God, he'll take me before I witness the death of anyone in my family." Then he walked into the living room and stood exactly where his life would be taken. He opened his arms and repeatedly said, "If there is a God, he will send a bomb right now to take my life. Take me God!"

"Stop saying that Robert," mom and I said.

"Well, you don't have to worry about that," Mom replied. "We'll all be safe in Egypt soon."

"If something happened to me, you'd all forget about me in three days," Robert said, as if he ignored what my mother had said a moment before.

"That's not true," I told him. "That's nonsense."

Three days later *(as I shared earlier)* my dad called our family into the living room for a meeting and said, "The country's situation is growing worse." We sat there, closely listening as he continued, "We all need to wrap things up soon and leave before the war breaks out."

After the family meeting was over, my parents went into the next room to listen to the radio, anxious to hear updates about the state of our country. My siblings left the house. Jacque went over to the next street to talk to a friend. Elie took Roger outside to fly paper airplanes.

Let me take you back to the time when Robert and I were sitting in the living room on that fateful day in 1975. We were having our great conversation about what I wanted to be when I grew up. In that particular moment when Robert wanted to get his tea from the kitchen, something told me, "Get up Aimmee. You need to get his tea." I didn't even realize what I was doing. I stood up quickly and headed towards the kitchen. "I'll get your tea, Robert," I said, with the same smile still on my face. "Then we can pick up where we left off. I'll be right back . . ."

As you know, the next few moments were when the bomb came through the window and took Robert's life. On that unforgettable day, I learned how important it is to be *present* and appreciate every moment I spend with my loved ones.

One of my most powerful realizations came to me *years* later. I discovered that every tragedy always holds many lessons to be learned and that each one is as valuable as hidden treasure.

*   *   *

After the incident, I was heartbroken to witness the rare occasion of heartfelt emotion from my mother. Soon after we had been whisked away from the smoldering building, weeping uncontrollably she cried out, "Thank you God that I only lost one child and not all of them," as she knelt and kissed the ground. At that moment, I felt guilty for wanting to be dead with Robert. It would hurt my mother to lose another child. That particular day, I felt my mom's pain and love at the same time. Unfortunately, tragedy can make children grow up fast. I know that's what it did for me.

Since everyone was caught up in the chaos, I had to step in, take charge of my life, and care for my little brother Roger. My love for him helped me to stay focused on what I had, NOT on what I had lost. I asked myself, "Do I want to focus on the problem and the chaos that's happening around me or do I want to *focus* on the *solution?*" The answer was obvious. Robert's tragedy pushed me to *challenge* myself and recognize the strength that we all have hidden inside.

*   *   *

The country's infrastructure had shut down over night, therefore we couldn't have a proper funeral for Robert. Taxis and buses stopped running. All of the roads were shut down. We had to stay on the run, moving to protected areas in order to avoid the bombs.

While moving from place to place, many neighbors opened up their homes and hearts to help us. Although the war was partly based on religious strife between Christian and Muslim officials, everyday Lebanese Muslims and Christians had generally gotten along fine.

Several years earlier, my dad's family purchased a burial site. It was located in the mountains in a new cemetery, which was still under construction. The surroundings were dismal, with piles of dirt all around and trash left behind by construction workers. Yet it was the only place we had to bury Robert, so that's where we laid his body to rest.

The roads leading to the cemetery had been closed until just days before the ceremony, so many family members, like my Aunt Nouhad, were unable to attend. Robert was so severely burned that he couldn't be dressed for burial and instead was wrapped in a white sheet. Right before he was taken away, my mom asked the undertaker to open up the coffin so that we could say goodbye. We saw him for less than three minutes, yet it felt like three hours.

Right then I started having flashbacks. The bombs, the smoke, the painfully loud noise, the confusion, the mayhem, the screaming, the crying, the disorientation, Mom almost jumping to her death—it all flashed right before my eyes. It was as if I was living the tragedy all over again and I started gasping for air. Burying Robert was heart wrenching for me. I couldn't handle seeing my family in such pain, knowing that I couldn't do anything to stop it.

As they were about to close the casket, I looked around at everyone feeling depressed and sad. My mom was so despondent she was shaking. She started hyperventilating and almost blacked out. For the first time ever, I saw my usually upbeat dad break down and cry, his face all red and swollen. Elie, on his hands and knees, cried out, "I love you brother." Roger, just six at the time, held his head down and sobbed. He was too young to fully understand what was going on and I wanted to be strong for him. Unfortunately in that moment, I couldn't be there for him. My heart and soul were shattered.

When the casket door was closed, part of me closed with it. As they lowered the coffin into the ground, we threw sand on it and were supposed to say our final goodbyes. I couldn't do it. I could never say goodbye to Robert.

Over thirty years later, it still hurts. I will never forget Robert. I don't think I will ever get over the anguish of seeing him die before my eyes, or witnessing his burned body laid to rest.

One thing I know for sure, I will *never* get over that horrible tragedy. Nor do I expect myself to do so. However, I know that I have the *power* over my thoughts and emotions to learn how to deal with it in a healthy way.

*   *   *

We not only lost Robert that day to the bomb, we also lost each other. The first couple of days we stayed at our neighbor's house, but then we had no choice and were forced to separate. No one had enough space for my entire family, so each of us stayed with different relatives or friends while mom and dad sorted out what to do next.

Dad's plan to sell his share of the factory had been put on hold. The investor didn't want to risk any more money since the war made the future of the country uncertain. As a result, the factory closed, leaving my dad with nothing to sell. Our hopes and dreams of moving to Egypt as a family vanished just like that.

As time went on, we started to stay with several members of my dad's family. We lived with my uncle Karim for a couple of weeks, and then I stayed with my grandfather Hagob and aunt in the mountains for about a month. Grandpa was a skinny, goodhearted man in his 80s. He was a hard worker and a good family man. He didn't speak much Arabic and I didn't speak Armenian, so we had trouble communicating, but he made a conscious effort to make me feel as comfortable as possible.

We'd sit on the balcony and talk as much as we could. He tried very hard to use all the Arabic he knew. When he asked me about Robert, I felt like I was going to burst. Grandpa was ill and getting on in age, so the family had decided to hide Robert's death from him, since they didn't think he would be able to handle the news. It was so hard for me to keep the secret. I desperately needed to talk to someone, anyone about it. Even though I didn't say anything, I think my body language tipped him off and he could sense that something was wrong. Every time Grandpa asked me about Robert, he noticed how nervous and fidgety I got, nearly jumping out of my chair. As a child, it was difficult to hide my emotions.

The only way I knew how to deal with them was to go to the other room and allow myself to cry and release the pain I felt. Through the tragedy of losing Robert, I learned how to balance my emotions. Even when I felt stuck in darkness, I could still lift myself up by seeing the *light* through my loved ones. I learned early on that it's okay to cry, but there comes a time when it's necessary to stop. This healthy approach helped me find balance and peace in my heart and mind. After releasing my emotions through my tears, I was able to walk out and handle having a conversation about Robert.

Every now and then Grandpa would say with love, "Here Aimmee. Take this and go buy some candy." That meant the world to me. I began to feel close to him as we started building a relationship. I was deeply saddened to learn about his death several months after I left. It was hard seeing my dad's sadness. In a short period of time he had buried his mother, his son Robert, and now his father. I assumed life couldn't get any worse . . . or so I thought.

CHAPTER FOUR

Determined To Keep My Spirit Up

So far I have introduced you to my family, and the beginning of the war. However, I haven't shared with you the life long lessons I learned as a child before my country went to war. From a very young age, I still remember one of the many lessons I learned from dad's wisdom. We often went to downtown Beirut together. Going there was a exciting treat for any kid and I loved spending time with dad. Walking by the interesting shops, we enjoyed the smells of the freshly baked breads and sweets. The air was filled with the constant chatter of farmers trying to sell their goods, while other people were haggling over prices. Simmering on hot skewers, vendors always had the best chicken and beef shawarmas (Lebanese gyros).

During one of our special trips together, I asked, "Dad, can you buy me shawarma?"

Unexpectedly, he replied, "Aimmee, I'm not going to buy you anything today."

"Why is that Daddy? I know you have money in your pocket," I asked with a confused and innocent look on my face.

"Just because I have money right now doesn't mean I always will", he responded. "You may not always be able to get what you want. I want to make sure that you understand that. Some days you may have a lot, and other days you might not." He continued sharing his wisdom, "Aimmee, you must learn how to deal with disappointments and stay happy at the same time."

Instead of getting upset, I understood what my dad was trying to teach. Seeing life differently helped me recognize and appreciate his insights. Even though I didn't get my way, his words lifted my spirit. I had learned a valuable lesson that helped me overcome many obstacles throughout life. Early on, I understood that whether you get what you want or *not*, true long term happiness always comes *from within*.

*   *   *

One day my parents decided to move to a bigger and better house. I was convinced that it would make life much easier. At least, that's what I thought. Shortly after moving in, we had a power outage. Jacque took advantage of the spooky atmosphere and turned this boring time into a fun and amusing experience. He took my baby brother Roger out on the balcony and started playing. It was dark and felt like Halloween Night.

Jacque yelled, "Come play with us Aimmee!"

"I don't feel like playing. I'm resting right now," I yelled back.

"Come on! Have fun with us," he begged.

"I helped clean the house all day. I'm tired! I don't feel like playing right now," I replied.

"You are way too young to be tired. Come on!" he hollered.

Finally, Jacque's enthusiasm beat out my tiredness and I gave in. When I was hurrying to the balcony to play with them, I hadn't realized which side of the sliding glass door was open. Earlier that day, its thin glass had been cleaned and was absolutely spotless and practically invisible. I was so tired that I couldn't even see straight and BOOM! I walked right into the sliding glass door. In between the room and the balcony, my body got stuck in the glass. Totally frightened and still unsure about what had happened, I went into shock.

Jacque jumped into action, pulled me away from the glass and carried me down to the first floor. He quickly got our neighbor, who was a taxi driver, and they frantically rushed me to the hospital. On the way there, I looked down and saw that one of my legs was open to the bone.

As soon as we got to the emergency room, the nurses immediately took me in and placed me on a bed in the ER. I started shivering and grew more scared when I realized how much blood I was covered in. A few minutes later, two doctors walked in. They spoke to each other in French and then began speaking Arabic to me. One doctor was very nice while the other one was exceptionally rude. I quickly became lost in a whirlwind of their conflicting demeanors and words . . .

The nice doctor asked, "What is your name honey?"

"Aimmee", I answered.

With a furrowed brow, the mean doctor asked me, "What were you thinking?" as he shook his head in disapproval.

"Don't be scared," the kind doctor chimed in.

"Why did you let this happen?", the unpleasant doctor continued with his criticism. I could feel his judgement.

As I was laying in the bed and they were working on my wounds, you would have thought that I was watching a tennis match. My head kept going back and forth as I was listening to each of them. In the back of my mind, I couldn't understand why the one doctor was being so mean.

The nice doctor quickly jumped in and asked, "Aimmee, would you do me a favor?"

"Yes," I answered as I shook my head.

With his comforting and soothing voice, he continued, "Good. Take a deep breath three times and relax." I did what he asked and he said, "Good girl."

With his deep voice, the unfriendly doctor said, "Next time, pay attention to what is going on around you." He was talking to me as if the accident were my fault.

Focusing on the doctors' conflicting messages tricked me into switching my attention from the pain to what they were saying.

They had to use over one hundred stitches to sew my legs, then, each leg was put in a cast. A night of fun had turned into an unpleasant memory.

The doctor told my mom to bring me back for cosmetic surgery. Since she was busy and had more than she could handle, she never had the chance to take me. To this day, the scars are still visible on my legs. Every time I see them they remind me of the lesson I learned from that incident. By playing their version of "good cop, bad cop", the doctors taught me a valuable lesson. At an early age, I started to understand the power of focus. They knew that if I was looking at and thinking about my legs or my pain, I would have been a difficult patient to deal with.

*　*　*

Emgalal, was our first fulltime nanny and had recently moved from Egypt to Lebanon. She was a middle-aged Egyptian lady with the shiniest and most beautiful dark skin. Her husband and kids were living in her home country. She felt so close to us, as we often reminded her of her own children. Even though mom and dad couldn't afford her, they felt that she would help ease the pressures of their stressful marriage.

My parents would leave sometimes for extended periods of time and forget to leave Emgalal with money, so the refrigerator and cabinets became nearly empty. They would leave thinking that everything was fine, but we would have gone hungry if it weren't for Emgalal's resourcefulness. She would make us something to eat from almost nothing. A soup of broken noodles and bouillon became our impromptu meal. She did her job the best she could but still could not take the place of an involved parent.

At times, when my brothers were fighting, Emgalal would get very frustrated. Who could blame her?

One day, she angrily said, "I'm going to leave you. I have no business being here. This is not my responsibility. I'm not even getting paid to take care of you. If you guys keep up this roughhousing, I'll definitely leave!"

These words and threats painfully ran through me. Without hesitation, I helplessly dropped on my knees. I grabbed Emgalal's legs, begging her, "Please don't leave! Don't leave Roger and me all alone!"

Fortunately, she decided not to quit. I felt that my prayers were answered. I knew that when she took a long vacation to visit family, that she was going to return to our home.

Even with Emgalal with us, I still felt the need to act like Roger's mom. Instead of doing things that normal kids would do, I focused on protecting my little brother. I always made sure that he was properly cared for.

Taking care of Roger filled me with joy and lifted my spirit. From a young age, I understood the power of giving and receiving! It is one of the most powerful cycles in life. The more you give, the more you receive. The more you receive, the more you *have* to give. Giving is an important part of living.

Unfortunately, my older brother Elie was not receiving the love he needed, therefore he was not able to give love. What he needed was something only mom could give, but she spent most of her time at work, visiting with friends, or trying to figure out how to deal with her own personal life.

Her being gone was something that he hated. He didn't know how to tell her that he wanted and needed her at home. Inside of him was a constantly building resentment and anger. When nobody was around, he would take it out on me. He associated me with mom and I was an easy target.

*   *   *

It was common for older siblings to punish their younger ones back then. Physical discipline was generally accepted, but Elie took things too far. He would watch me like a hawk, just waiting for me to make a mistake so his disciplining me could be justified. He didn't just spank me like a parent might spank a toddler. His methods of abuse took various forms. He pushed me into corners and beat me mercilessly. At times, he grabbed me by the hair, pulling out wads with his hands. He often threw me against the wall, which resulted in goose egg sized bumps on my head that stayed well-hidden by my hair. He continued to find new ways to torment me.

Since I hadn't walked for several months after my glass door accident, my legs had grown weak. Soon after my casts were removed, he angrily came after me. While I was still in bandages, he pulled me down to the floor by grabbing my hair. Emgalal came home and found me there crying.

"What happened?" she asked me.

"That's what she gets for trying to get up and walk around," Elie growled, answering for me. "The doctor told her to wait several more weeks. Her legs aren't ready for walking yet."

I was so hurt, hearing his piercing words. Not only was he beating me, but he was also covering it up by blaming me for trying to walk.

From time to time, the neighbors would come over to see what was going on when they heard my cries. Since all of the houses in Beirut are very close together, everyone knew everybody else's business. You could bet that if something was going on in your house, your neighbors knew about it.

As my screams filled the house one day, there was a knock on the door. I'll never forget that moment. I felt like someone was coming to rescue me. As Elie opened the door, the neighbor asked, "Everyone all right here?"

Elie slyly replied back, "Yeah, everything is fine. She's not doing what she's supposed to do. I'm just disciplining her. You know how kids are sometimes. They just never listen. If they're not disciplined, they'll run wild."

The neighbor thought that everything was in order so he never intervened and quickly left. Since I wasn't doing what I was supposed to do, I deserved whatever punishment I got. I took the opportunity while he was talking to the neighbor and gave myself a break to breathe. Curling my body up gave me the illusion of safety. I looked like a turtle going into its shell trying to find an escape and protection. Hiding in the corner while in that position, I began to cry uncontrollably, only catching my breath in between sobs.

Considering the situation, I was still able to gather the courage and strength within. I boldly asked him, "What did I do, Elie? Why are you hitting me?"

He yelled back, "You were a bad girl! Look, I can't believe you made such a mess. Can't you see the water on the floor? Do you see all the crumbs all over the rug?"

As I walked away, I said, "I'll clean it all up. You didn't have to hit me like that!"

Soon, we repeatedly started moving from one apartment to another. I don't know if my parents were running from their problems or if they believed moving would somehow improve their marriage. Regardless, no matter where we lived, they continued to fight and argue. This type of instability made Elie's nonstop frustrations only worse. He seemed to always be looking for ways to crush my spirit. I did not want to tell my parents about the abuse since it would only give them another thing to fight about. When my parents were running away from their problems, they weren't able to be *present* with their kids.

*   *   *

My father and I naturally connected well. He was a good teacher and I was a good listener. Dad noticed that I started to have some resentment towards my mom. I wanted her to give more attention to Elie. Every time he picked up on my feelings, he would say, "Aimmee, resentment *poisons* your body, spirit and mind."

Hearing those words from my dad helped me open my heart and eyes. From that moment on, every time I felt resentment towards my mom, Elie or someone at school, I made sure to turn it *into* compassion. I was determined not to allow anyone to crush my spirit!

This insight from my dad helped prepare me for the tests I would have to face in the difficult years ahead . . .

CHAPTER FIVE

My New Best Friend

Robert was the only one of my older siblings I felt close to. I appreciated every little bit of attention and love he gave me. Every once in a while Robert would say, "Come on Aimmee, let's go have fun." I loved it when he used to surprise me and take me to the beach. I was especially excited when he would take me to my favorite place to see a movie, Concorde Theatre. I loved riding on the back of his motorcycle and feeling the wind on my face. "Go faster!" I would yell to him gleefully. "Hold on tight. Here we go!" he'd say. Then he'd speed up, dashing and darting around curves trying to scare me just enough to make the ride even more fun and exciting. I felt so happy and carefree during those liberating moments on the back of my brother's bike. I didn't think about my parents' arguments, Elie's beatings, or having to play mother to Roger, until one day, when we returned from an outing to discover that Roger had been injured.

He had been up on the balcony talking to some children playing in the street when he fell ten feet down to the ground below. Fortunately, his fall was broken by a clothing line and softened by a rug that fell with him from above. He wasn't badly hurt, but I felt guilty for having gone to the movies with Robert. I thought if I had been watching him carefully, as I usually did, the whole incident would never have happened.

I truly believe that our experiences in life shape us into who we are today.

As a child, the feeling and the possibility of losing my brother was overwhelming. That thought taught me to *appreciate* every moment I have with my family, and encouraged me to be close to them and always tell them how much I love them.

* * *

I was eight years old when my mom told me that I was going to be sent to a boarding school. Even with my family's financial difficulties and the fact it wasn't affordable, mom sent me away. One less child at home lightened her load. All the money she earned went toward my tuition.

Boarding school took me away from the two women I admired most in my life, my Grandma Esma and my Aunt Nouhad. Both were from my mother's side of the family. I loved visiting them. Since they lived next to each other, it was easy for me to go back and forth between houses during visits. Being with them gave me a welcome break from Elie. I always wished I could live with Grandma or Aunt Nouhad. When I was with either of them, I never wanted to leave. They were amazing women and I truly looked up to them.

Grandma Esma always greeted me with affection and love. I remember her one bedroom apartment. She had a small bed, a sofa and a tiny dining table and an old fashioned wooden clock. Her apartment was nothing like ours. It was quiet and peaceful. I used to lay down on her sofa while she was cooking and I listened to the clock until I fell asleep. She would wake me saying, "Aimmee, get up! The food is ready." Those were very good memories.

Aunt Nouhad was like a mom to me. I admired how she took such good care of her family and showed her love by putting them first. I loved everything about her home including the house rules she established, such as only eating in the dining area. Her home was infused with good energy and wonderful love. They had kids close to my age and there were plenty of toys.

As you know, studying was very difficult for me. I was failing year after year at school, which had strict academic standards. If you didn't score high enough on the year-end exams, you weren't allowed to advance to the next grade. Since I was falling behind, I became one of the oldest and tallest kids in the class. This made me stick out even more. My assigned seat was in the back of the classroom. Whenever it was my turn to read aloud, it was a dreadful nightmare. This task, which was easy for most students, caused me to offer up frantic prayers to God. *Please let the bell ring soon! Make the teacher skip over me! Get him to start a different activity! Please help me!* Due to my trouble with reading, I couldn't understand assignments. Learning any subject was becoming an increasing struggle and I desperately needed one on one attention.

I was ridiculed by students. My lack of fluency in reading caused kids to treat me like an outcast. Kids my age didn't want to play with me since I wasn't in the same grade as them.

Sitting in the back didn't help my study habits or reading ability, but it helped me make a powerful discovery. Since I didn't have any friends, I had a lot of time to learn about my emotions. By connecting with my feelings, I discovered I had the choice to become my own best friend, someone who would care for me. I felt loved and warm from the inside. It was a feeling I couldn't describe. I was able to block out most of the negative thoughts by spending much of my time with my newly created best friend.

Despite all the teasing and taunting, I knew my own level of intelligence. I had the ability to see things and interpret information in a different way. Unfortunately, my dyslexia directly interfered with my schooling. The awareness of my problem didn't come until later in life. "Wow!" I said to myself one day, "This whole time I've been wondering why I couldn't do what other kids could. Finally the source of my difficulties in school has a name."

Every time I heard my father tell me, "Aimmee, you are a smart girl. Anyone can go to school and learn, but not everyone has your intelligence. You should feel blessed by what God gave you." I didn't know what to think. I wondered if he was just telling me that because he felt I needed to hear it. At times, I was puzzled and simply didn't know how to feel. After all, I was just a kid who was getting confused between the words of my best friend, my father, and those who were trying to crush my spirit.

Regardless of my learning disability, I was always insightful and perceptive, absorbing everything around me. Unfortunately, at school, my measure of intelligence was overlooked and I was unfairly labeled as a lazy student.

Unlike dad, mom often accused me of being stupid. She tried to help me in her own way, believing that if she pushed me hard enough, I would become better at school. Some parents in my culture, like my mom, use unhealthy techniques in an attempt to motivate their children. Mom didn't know how to encourage me to be a better student without saying hurtful things. Soon, it wasn't enough for her to compare me to Jacqueline, she began comparing me to anyone she could think of. This pushed me further into my shell, preventing me from speaking up for myself.

*   *   *

My parents weren't always able to make payments to the boarding school. When they didn't, I'd have to clean to pay for my tuition. It was so embarrassing to be pulled off the playground and away from the other kids, who already laughed and jeered at me for being held back from my class. This gave my schoolmates even more opportunities to tease me. My self-esteem had already been shattered by Elie's abuse and it was completely destroyed the first time I was forced to clean.

One day as I was cleaning the second floor of the school, I heard the sound of a familiar engine. I looked and saw a tall young man getting off his motorcycle. As he was taking off his helmet, I realized that it was Robert! When I saw his face, the sadness I felt was instantly replaced with the happiness growing within me. I wanted to jump up and down with joy. Knowing that someone from my family cared enough to visit was exciting and completely cheered me up. During those visits, Robert became my hero.

After Robert worked out the tuition payments, I was given permission to play with the other kids again. However, none of them wanted to play with me. Even before my cleaning duty, the upscale school's rich kids looked down on me and thought I was beneath them.

My struggles weren't through. Fitting in continued to be a hurtful problem. It was embarrassing to wear hand-me-downs while the other kids were sporting new clothes in the latest styles. My shy and quiet nature didn't help me in the matter.

The hardest part of attending that school was missing my younger brother Roger. *Who was going to take care of him when Emgalal was on one of her long vacations visiting her family? Who was watching him when my parents were fighting?* Somehow, I still felt responsible for him. As I walked alone around the school grounds, I hoped that somehow he was being properly cared for.

*   *   *

One day, I told Robert about how the kids were treating me and how no one would play with me. A week later, he came for another visit.

"Here. I brought this ball thinking you could make friends and play with the other kids," he said happily. He had always been so thoughtful.

"Oh! Thank you! This is great. I can't wait to use it. You're the best!" I replied with a smile.

Holding the ball close to my heart with both arms, I headed toward the playground thinking to myself, *"I finally have my ticket to play with the other girls."* When I got there, I was approached by the most popular girl in school. All the other girls followed her. They surrounded me as if it was time for show and tell.

She asked, "Can I see the ball? It looks really new!"

Before I could think of any specific words, I anxiously blurted out, "Of course! My brother just gave it to me." Then, I handed it to her.

I excitedly thought to myself, *"Finally, after all this waiting, they're going to play with me. They're letting me in their inner circle."* I confidently approached them, eager to start playing. Then, the unwelcome moment of truth came. They weren't going to play with me. Even Robert's thoughtful idea didn't work. I was still the outcast. Left out of the fun, I plopped down on an old green bench nearby feeling unwanted and defeated. Watching them play with my new ball without me made my wounds deeper.

The rejection from my schoolmates was very painful. However, my imaginary best friend would always remind me of my father's insightful words, "Aimmee, resentment *poisons* your body, spirit and mind."

*   *   *

My best friend was there for me and protected me every step of the way, not only at school, but also at home when my parents were fighting over the simple things.

Mom had a bad habit. She never screwed the caps back on to the bottle tops. It didn't matter if she was drinking water, soda or taking medication from a bottle. For some reason, she would not put in the effort required for such a common, simple task. This annoying little habit would drive my dad crazy. He would get so frustrated. Whenever he got mad, it seemed like all of his wisdom went out the window.

One day, my dad grabbed a bottle of soda to take a drink. Since the cap was not on, the bottle fell to the floor. It shattered into a thousand little pieces and splattered all over his dress pants. He angrily screamed, "Why can't you just close the damn thing Antoinette?"

I didn't hear my mother answer, however I saw her usual response of shrugging her shoulders in an "I don't care" manner and walking away. She headed out the door, off to who-knows-where. She would be gone for several hours, and sometimes for days. This was how she generally reacted when they argued.

The only way I knew how to deal with these episodes was to go to a different apartment building and sit on the steps with the neighbors' kids. I tried to get my mind off of my parents' troubles as we played with the little family of dolls that we made out of ice cream sticks. We crossed two of the little pieces of wood together and tied them with sewing thread. Tiny buttons are what we used for the eyes and scraps of material were used for the clothing.

"Time for dinner! Come on," yelled one girl's mom. Off she went, leaving to go eat with her family.

"See you later Aimmee."

"Bye," I said, with a weak smile.

Later on, I heard, "Time for you to come in! It's getting dark," from another friend's mother. We said our quick goodbyes and she left.

One by one, the kids left since it was either getting dark or it was dinnertime. I sat there alone. I wished one of my family members had remembered me but they were wrapped up in their issues. I waited for someone to call me, but it rarely happened. I had a house, but I felt as if I had no home. Everyone left, except for my newly created best friend. She jumped in and helped me have peace in my heart and mind by simply being there. This scenario repeated almost every time my parents fought.

My best friend didn't leave me then and she never has. I'm grateful that at least I had her because I had no idea that life was going to become harder and that I'd need her *more than ever* . . .

CHAPTER SIX

Reaching For Answers

"We can't afford your tuition anymore this year so you're going to be placed in a different boarding school," said mom. I was around nine years old.

It was time to get back to school and mom started preparing everything I needed. When the time came, she got a taxi and we headed toward the mountain where the school was located. When we arrived, she went to the principal's office and I waited outside. A few moments later she came out and said, "It's time to leave. I need to drop off your luggage and show you where you are going to sleep."

The school had two buildings connected to each other, one for girls and one for boys. As we were walking toward my new living quarters, I looked around and I could see some of the classrooms through the windows. The old paint on the walls was chipping off and half of the seats were broken. To my left, I noticed that the playground was not like the one at my other school. This one was dirty and run down. We finally came to the room where I'd be staying. I could see the unhappy look on my mom's face, but there was nothing she could do about it. We were already there and this school was the only option.

The room was set up almost like a military camp. It had a large room with at least fifty beds lined up next to each other. They were so close together that it was hard to move between them. Each girl was assigned a bed with an old mattress that had broken metal springs.

We walked to the end of the large room where a lady was sitting, drinking Turkish coffee. She introduced herself as Miss Emhany and invited my mom to sit down so they could talk. My new housemother told mom about the school guidelines. She then highlighted the rules for the room where I'd be staying, which was the one she oversaw. Next she showed me where I was going to sleep and said, "Go ahead and put your luggage underneath your bed Aimmee. You need to do that if you want support for your back while you sleep. It will also keep the bed from collapsing." This was the moment that I clearly understood that this experience was going to be worse than my first boarding school.

Miss Emhany was an unhappy woman who wore her problems on her sleeve. She was a divorcee with several children who received no financial support from her ex-husband. Even though she didn't make much money, she provided an education and shelter for her family in exchange for her work at the school. Since she couldn't hear well, every time she spoke it was exceptionally loud. To me, it sounded like she was yelling. We had to speak just as loud if we wanted her to hear us. Since I was a very quiet kid, raising my voice to talk to her made me very uncomfortable. The loud talking between Miss Emhany and the kids reminded me of the noisy, constant chaos in my household.

My bed wetting problem I had experienced at home for a long time continued at school. I would often wake up in the morning embarrassed since my mattress and I were smelly and wet. My bed was in the middle of the room so I couldn't hide my accidents. The other girls would point at me and laugh when they found out. I didn't know what to do and was too timid to ask Miss Emhany or anyone else for help. Since we received clean sheets only once a week, I had to sleep with the stench of urine until the next linen day came around. I had always been the clean, meticulous type, so having to sleep on pee-stained stinky sheets was very disturbing. More than anything else, this emotionally-draining problem diminished what little confidence I had and was completely humiliating. I kept thinking to myself, *"Aimmee, if you stay awake you can control this.*

Don't fall asleep!" Doing my very best was all I could do and by knowing that, it helped me have some peace in my heart.

I figured that my bed wetting was going to be the only problem I had to deal with. I was wrong. Every day of living at the school I discovered something new. There was a variety of things that I had to deal with and accept. The food was given to us in small portions and tasted awful. Many times, I decided to skip meals to avoid eating the food. Seeing rats run across the floor in the kitchen didn't help my appetite either.

Hygiene was something that I was pretty sure did not exist in the school's vocabulary. The lice situation was out of control. Almost all of us had it at least once during our tenure there. Miss Emhany would take us into the bathroom one by one and sit us on her lap. She'd yank a small comb through small sections of our hair to remove the lice. If we even blinked at all, she would hold us firmly and scream "Don't move!" Even when the pulling hurt, we just had to sit there until she was done.

We then had to go to a small shower room which was also the girls' bathroom. The tiny space could only hold Miss Emhany and two other kids. Sitting in the room was a propane tank which heated a large cylinder of water that was three feet high and very wide. The top of it was open so we could see the water and and the flame heating it underneath was visible. Miss Emhany would sit on an old stool next to the boiling water. Using a large bowl, she would mix the hot water with the cold to lower the temperature. Then she poured it on our heads. After having our hair pulled on so much just a few minutes before, our heads were still very tender. The hot water was painful and felt like it was burning our scalps.

Difficulties with my schoolwork continued. It became very hard for me to study and focus. I was worried about my family, preoccupied about dealing with bullies, and I continued to struggle with reading difficulties. As a result, my grades continued to plummet and it became increasingly difficult for me to complete my homework. In those days, teachers were allowed to physically discipline students and the punishment for undone homework was getting spanked on the fingers with a metal ruler. On a regular basis, I could always count on getting whacked.

If my family didn't come to see me each week, the other kids would make fun of me. I would go to sleep praying that someone would show up. Finally, one day my older sister Jacqueline and her family visited. I could see them coming up the hill through the big screen door that locked us in the school like prisoners. Seeing them made me so happy.

Most families would take their kids home for the weekend or holidays. At times when my parents were busy fighting or temporarily separated, they did not pick me up from boarding school. The only kids there during those times were Miss Emhany, her children and me. It was hard having her around day and night and seeing her more often than my own family.

The only nice thing about being at that school was the balcony. The view of Beirut was beautiful. I used to imagine reaching out and being at the ocean. I loved the beach and enjoyed swimming. Even though it was just a daydream, it felt wonderful simply seeing the ocean and thinking about being there.

*　　*　　*

Every once in a while, mom made arrangements for me to take a taxi back to our apartment in Beirut. When it was time for me to leave boarding school for a holiday vacation, I felt both happy and scared. I was always excited to see my family, yet facing Elie and my parents fighting stirred up a lot of unhealthy emotions.

As you know, my household was challenging. Whenever I went back, my older brother Elie's abuse would start back up. I dreaded his actions so much that I wanted to return to my awful school. I desperately wanted to confide in someone about Elie, but was confused about whether or not I should tell anyone. I was constantly scared and wondering why mom and dad couldn't see what was happening. Their situation was also getting worse. Telling on Elie would only complicate things. I kept telling myself, *"This is not the right time Aimmee. It is safer to keep things to yourself. Stay in your shell. Just stuff your emotions. You can handle it.*

Can't you see how much dad is trying to make his marriage work?" Making excuses was easier than speaking up.

Even if they had argued just moments before, dad would attempt to change the atmosphere by serving my mom breakfast; anything to create peace. "Wake up, princess," he'd say as he knocked on the bedroom door. "Wake up." Then he would bring her a tray with coffee, juice, and perhaps *manaeesh* (a baked dough brushed with olive oil and sprinkled with *zatar*, a spiced blend of thyme, sesame seeds, and other spices). No matter what my father did, I always felt the power of my mom's resentment toward him.

Whether she recognized it or not, resentment was following her like a shadow, poisoning her spirit and mind and crushing her family.

*   *   *

While I was at school, mom's salon business closed. In an effort to pay for my tuition and escape her troubled marriage, she decided to take a job as housemother at my boarding school. Part of her duties included cleaning the boys' living quarters. It came as no surprise that she could not handle the job. How could she when she couldn't even handle the responsibility of her own children? It was hard for me to see my mother sad, confused and distraught. She was going through a major bout of depression and was overwhelmed with work. I stepped in and took as many of her responsibilities as I could so she could keep her job. The best part of having mom at school was the fact that she brought Roger with her.

The boys' living quarters was always a mess and having to clean it was gross and difficult. For a young girl my age, it was also very awkward. I couldn't dare say anything about how dirty it was to them or my mom. The boys were mean, aggressive and severely ridiculed me. Tears would pour down my face when they would push me around and call me names.

Unable to run away from her problems forever, mom soon returned to Beirut with Roger. When they left, I was crushed. Having Roger there helped me cope with the darkness permeating the school. Cleaning for mom had also allowed me to occasionally avoid spending time in class. I liked cleaning much better, yet I got even further behind in my lessons.

*   *   *

After returning to school from a holiday break, I spent the first week back as the only student punished for incomplete homework. One day my teacher walked over to me and asked, "Did you hurt yourself Aimmee?" and pointed to the bruise that just barely showed from beneath my short sleeved shirt.

"Yes sir, I fell," I mumbled. The bruises were from my brother Elie's beatings.

"Hmmm. That's a funny place to land. What happened?"

"Um, well . . .," I said nervously. He had caught me totally off guard. I was surprised that he noticed the bruise in the first place, and I couldn't drum up an explanation quickly enough to sound convincing. My heart began to swell up inside me, pounding away like hail hitting the pavement.

While the teacher stared at me, I started to lose my composure and began to cry. I couldn't hold back my anguish any longer. I had to let my skeleton out of the closet and thought that just maybe I could trust him. After all, he was a teacher. I assumed that you could always trust your teachers.

"My brother beat me," I mumbled.

"That's horrible," he said. "A pretty girl like you shouldn't have to endure such dreadful behavior. Surely, if you told your parents, they would put a stop to that at once."

"No sir, you don't understand. I don't want them to know," I replied.

"Don't worry. It's okay. Your secret's safe with me and you're safe here," he said, as he put his arms around me to console me. Although it was somewhat awkward having a man who was not my father or some other relative embracing me, at that moment I felt protected and safe.

The following week, I was again the only student sent to detention. Upon arriving, I grabbed a desk, pulled out my unfinished homework and pretended to start working. After all, the reason I wasn't doing my homework was that it was too difficult for me, which is why I was in detention in the first place.

The teacher, after finishing the paperwork he was engrossed in, noticed that I was just shuffling my papers about and not really getting any work done. He got up, locked the door, and approached my desk.

"Is there a problem?" he asked.

"Yes, sir. I'm having trouble with my school work," I explained. "That's why I'm being sent to detention. I can't do it on my own."

"I can help you," he said, "but you cannot tell anyone about it. I will help you with whatever troubles you, my child."

It seemed a bit strange that he didn't want me to tell anyone about his willingness to help. I wondered, "Why would anyone want to hide something nice like that?" Yet I was happy that someone, anyone wanted to help me. I agreed not to say anything about his help and no sooner than I did, he grabbed my hand and caressed my face. I was utterly confused and knew what he was doing wasn't right. I desperately desired attention, but I quickly realized that I didn't want that kind.

"Remember, you can't tell anyone about this," he said abruptly, just as detention was about to end. "I'd hate to have to tell your parents that your brother is hitting you."

My heart sank to the bottom of the Dead Sea. Even though I was too young and naive to fully understand what was going on, I knew that whatever was happening was not good. Just as it dawned on me that he was holding my deep secret over my head—the knowledge of a family skeleton I wanted to remain in the closet—the dismissal bell rang. I quickly got up and left.

From that moment on, I tried my best to stay on top of my schoolwork in order to stay out of detention, but the pressure only made matters worse. The fear of going to detention made it difficult for me to concentrate on my studies, so I ended up serving detention for unfinished assignments at least once a week for the rest of my time at that school.

With each visit, the teacher's behavior became increasingly inappropriate and I became more and more ashamed of it as time went on. I grew more burdened at school and wanted to go home. Yet I knew when I got home, Elie would beat me and then I'd want to return to school. I was so confused. I felt like I should never confide in anyone ever again.

Two secrets now had me trapped, Elie's beatings and the teacher's immoral actions. Whenever things got too hard for me to handle, I did the exact same thing. I crawled inside a closet and sat curled up in the back corner, hidden beneath the clothes with the door shut. It felt like the closet was my only true escape.

Resentment was taking over my emotions and my life. I resented everyone, including myself. Out of my pain, I started searching for answers and then it hit me. My father's words came back, *"Aimmee, resentment will crush you and poison your spirit."* He was right. That's exactly what it was doing.

In my experience, pain always made me stronger. It helped me to become a fighter. Every time I felt pain in my heart I STOOD UP for myself and I refused to give in. By taking a deep breath and quietly closing my eyes, I was able to meditate and pray to God for strength. Doing so helped me to turn my *resentment into reconnecting* with my soul and spirit.

What I learned during my childhood days helped me face the difficult battles ahead . . .

CHAPTER SEVEN

The War Continued

Despite my father's best efforts, his plans fell through. He was unable to sell his factory and my oldest brother Jacque also lost his business. My family quickly became homeless and separated. We didn't have enough money for the whole family to travel to Egypt, so my father and Jacque went by themselves, leaving the rest of us behind. Their goal was to see if they could develop new businesses there. Elie and mom stayed with grandma Esma. Roger and I went to Miss Emhany at the boarding school in the mountains until my parents got situated and were able to take us back.

Although our family life had been stressful most of the time with my parents always arguing and Elie's abuse, I knew in my heart that I would miss everyone. I would have taken all the arguing and hitting in the world if it would have kept my entire family together. I didn't want to lose anyone else. As we were dropped off at school, I begged them not to go and leave us there. When the car drove away, my heart went with them. The only hope we had was the possibility of one day being back together.

Soon after that, the road from Beirut to the mountains was closed and the phones lines in the area were shut down due to damage from the bombing. Everyone at the school lost all contact with their family members and there was no way for them to reach us. To make matters worse, vehicles were no longer able to deliver food. The hardest part for me was seeing my baby brother Roger digging through the trash cans to find scraps of food.

The school couldn't afford a janitor anymore and was quickly becoming unlivable. Garbage wasn't being picked up and the kitchen wasn't being cleaned. We were sure to die of famine or disease if the bombs didn't kill us first.

The playground restrooms were gross and unsanitary. A few of us had to take turns cleaning them since the water system was down and the toilets were already full, the ground outside became our toilet. Used toilet paper was scattered all over the ground. Since there was no new toilet paper, we had to find used scraps of old newspapers and magazines.

Every time it was my turn to clean the restrooms, I would feel a pain in my stomach and would usually end up vomiting. I remember having to carefully step over the feces to avoid getting my shoes dirty. I had to pinch my nose to avoid the stench while flies buzzed around my head.

Not having proper sanitary conditions, I became infected with intestinal worms. When I first made this discovery, I was horrified and scared to death. However, it was so embarrassing that I didn't tell anyone.

With the water supply limited, most of the time we couldn't take proper showers. We'd use the bathroom, but couldn't wash our hands. The smell of garbage drifted through the air and flies were everywhere. Many of the kids were getting sick.

It didn't take long before there wasn't enough food for breakfast. For lunch, we'd stand in a single file line on the playground. One at a time, we'd approach the table where they'd hand us either an apple or a palm-sized piece of bread with a little bit of tomato paste on top. We were so hungry that we'd start eating right away. The food would be gone before we had a chance to sit down. I wanted to make sure that Roger had enough food to eat, so I began giving him my lunches. This made me hungrier than usual. I couldn't wait until dinner because it was the only meal I ate. I felt like I was Roger's mother more than ever before.

Dinner was usually the same as lunch. Every now and then, the cook was able to find a wild chicken roaming the area and we were treated to the delicacy of chicken soup.

As much as I wanted to play with the other kids, I didn't since I was grieving. Even if they had asked me to play, I wouldn't have. I simply wasn't emotionally available. Despite the war and the poor conditions at the school, everyone else was playing. Roger and I were two of only a handful of kids who had lost a loved one in those early days of the war. All I could think about was the loss of Robert and how the rest of my family was doing.

I would sit on a concrete block on the playground with my back against a tree. Looking up at the sky, I'd talk to God. That was the beginning of my ever-deepening relationship with Him. God became my family and my friend.

I had never fit in with the other kids. While the other girls were wearing their normal clothes on the weekends, I was wearing black to respect my brother's death. I not only felt different, but I also looked different. On top of that, I was taller than most of the girls my age and my body was rapidly developing.

At night, I would sneak out of bed, climb on to the balcony, and watch the war down in the city below. I could see the bombs flying across the sky like balls of fire. It was horrible knowing that the rest of my family was in the midst of that danger.

I took each bomb personally, believing that each one was going to hurt someone in my family. *That one's going to hit mom. That one will hit my brother,* I thought. I lived in fear and constantly wondered, *Who else am I going to lose?*

Every night I would pray to God, asking Him to help me stay strong for my little brother and to keep the rest of my family safe. I would also pray for Robert's soul. God was the only one I could talk to about my pain. Talking to Him was peaceful and gave me a chance to take a breath.

I did my best to stay strong for Roger, but I was never the same after seeing Robert die right before my eyes. I was paranoid and didn't like to be alone. I never received any emotional therapy and had to deal with his death by myself. At the tender age of twelve, I started having emotional breakdowns and nightmares.

My parents had to worry about keeping us safe and alive, so it was understandable that providing emotional support for me, and the rest of us, was the furthest thing from their minds. In those days, it wasn't common for people to seek emotional and psychological help to deal with their issues. Most people just dealt with things the best they could. I would tell myself, *"Aimmee, turn your fear into faith. When I did that, I felt the weight lift off of my shoulders."*

*   *   *

Several months later, the road to the school finally opened again. I was so relieved when I saw my mother. She was alive! I felt like the happiest girl on the planet seeing mom for the first time in months. I was jumping up and down with joy and then ran to embrace her. I happily discovered that mom was somewhat more stable and was so excited when Roger and I got in the car to leave with her, headed back to Beirut. Having this new sense of security meant the world to me. My family had moved into an empty house across the street from my uncle. The house was still under construction when the war started, so there was no electricity or running water. The walls had not yet been painted and the floor was just a foundation. We got some blankets from my uncle and we slept on flattened cardboard boxes. Despite the extreme modesty of our new home, for Roger and me, it was like a palace compared to the conditions we experienced at the boarding school. We were also happy to be with our family again.

My uncle and the neighbors gave us water to fill several buckets and our bathtub so that we could wash dishes and bathe. The sun provided light during the day and we used candles at night. We had only the clothes on our backs and whatever people could spare to give us.

About a month later, dad returned from Egypt while Jacque stayed there. The moment I saw dad, I took a huge deep breath. I hadn't felt such security and warmth in a long time. With a huge smile, I ran to him and gave him the biggest hug ever. I finally felt like I was home. This was the most complete my family had been since the war started. Confiding in my father was so easy for me. I trusted him completely. I told him about the intestinal worms. He could tell that I was embarrassed and scared. "Aimmee, don't worry about it. I will take care of it." Later, he gave me some medicine that helped me get better.

Meanwhile, the war was still going on and people were dying left and right. Suffering was everywhere, yet mom blamed dad for everything that happened. She thought he should have gotten the whole family out of Lebanon in time and that he should have had more money to take care of us. I sat back and watched them argue about something that happened in the past. If they had stopped arguing and started talking about possible solutions, I'm sure they could have *combined their power* and solved our current problems.

*   *   *

Lebanon's history reaches back to the beginnings of mankind. Like any Old World country, it is filled with thousands of years of traditions and customs. With its blend of Old World culture and modern day sophistication, Beirut had often been called "The Paris of the Middle East." The nickname was also given as a result of the French occupation of Lebanon during the early 20th century, which left evidence of its influence everywhere; in the architecture, food, language, and clothing.

When I was a kid, a person's worth was measured by the reputation of his or her family. The people kept good verbal records from generation to generation. What your father did before you, and what his father did before him all mattered. What your mother did before you and what her mother did before her mattered just as much.

Back in those days, Middle Eastern women were expected to wear all black for two years after the death of a child or spouse. Even during the summer, women would not leave home without black nylons if they had recently buried a loved one. Men didn't shave for at least a week.

Life all but stopped and no weddings or engagements could take place for at least the first year.

Two years of mourning is a long time. Mom couldn't handle the normal day to day stress, so the war brought on a huge amount of new pressures. She had lost her son, her house and her source of income. On top of that, she was expected to adhere to cultural norms of wearing black for two years while she was trying to protect her kids from the bombings. All of these burdens pushed her to the fine line between sanity and insanity. She started taking antidepressants like many other Middle Easterners did during that period in order to help her cope with the pain. She quickly developed a dependence on the drugs.

The period after losing Robert was one of mom's darkest times, as dark as the black clothing she was expected to wear day after day. It was difficult to see her so depressed and hopeless.

*   *   *

I was around thirteen years old when friends and extended family members began blessing my family and helping us along. My father's good friends, Abed and Dolee, opened their hearts and their home to us. We were able to stay there safely and comfortably for several weeks. It was amazing being able to have full meals, take showers and drink clean water everyday.

My father's relative Serope lived in the same neighborhood and helped us get into an available apartment. It was a small one room and one bath unit with very little furniture. Despite being used to living in a larger home, this tiny apartment was still a blessing. We didn't have to move around anymore for a while. Even though we were struggling financially, the stability was wonderful. For several weeks, Serope and his family helped us as much as they could, inviting us to eat with them. I became very good friends with his daughters Maral and Azad.

After we settled into the apartment, mom, Elie, Roger, and I stayed behind while dad left again to look for work and business opportunities. He hoped to send for us soon. From time to time, mom would break down. She needed somewhere to direct her anger and would spew all the bad feelings she harbored toward my father on me because I was so close to him.

Elie was much worse. He was deeply distraught about Robert's death. Just two years apart in age, he and Elie were best friends. Elie had a hard time coping with Robert's death and our mother's grief. He had always been so close to mom and couldn't handle seeing her depressed. His sadness turned to pain, his pain turned to more anger, which led to fits of rage. Consequently, after Robert's death, Elie would beat me even worse than he had before.

The war was still running its course. Bombs were destroying everything. We would go without consistent electricity or running water for up to three months at a time. We had to become creative in dealing with everyday life.

Families who could afford it would use a generator to pump water up to large buckets on the roof during the couple of hours we might have power throughout the day. That way, when the electricity would die, we'd be able to have running water as long as the bucket wasn't dry. Every drop of water was precious. Sometimes we'd go to sleep thirsty. We even used the water from bathing to clean the floor.

We couldn't even bathe in peace. When we took a shower, we'd have to keep a robe or some clothes nearby, just in case the bombs would start falling. We were not safe anywhere or at any time.

During power outages, the girls my age would gather to watch TV in one of the units with a generator. Despite the harshness of the war, we cherished making popcorn and sitting around chatting. The war brought families and neighbors together, one household helping another. We were all one big family.

When the lights would come back on after a long outage of electricity, everyone would shout with joy. You could hear all the cheering from blocks away. It was like the excitement of a big sporting event when the favored team made a point. Everyone would give each other high fives and hugs. Positive energy was everywhere. We were so appreciative just to have lights again, even for a few hours. When this happened, it always gave us hope. Hope is *"Having Open Possibilities Everyday."* It's extremely important to always keep hope alive.

* * *

While we were settling down in the tiny apartment, the cease fire had started. This was a welcome break from the chaos. The war soon quickly started back up closer to our neighborhood, forcing us to leave the apartment for the time being and seek safety somewhere else.

We were regularly on the move trying to escape the bombs and just trying to stay alive. We soon lost communication with dad, Jacque, and Jacqueline. We also had no money coming in. Mom would sit all day with her head hung down, trying to figure out what to do next. When things got to be too much for her, she'd leave and go to the neighbors.

We would eat nothing but soup for days. Roger and I had become accustomed to eating next to nothing when we were at school, but mom had a really hard time dealing with that. She had always wanted to get back to the "good life" my parents experienced before my father gave up his salon business. But the war crushed her dreams for a better life. She became even more depressed and emotionally withdrawn.

Elie had always been a lot like mom. He couldn't handle pressure well and as a result, he became increasingly angry and uncontrollable. I would walk on eggshells around him, trying to deflect his anger by being extra nice to him, in hopes that he wouldn't lose it. I knew deep down that Elie had a good heart. I hadn't been a good student, but I was always perceptive and good in dealing with reality and life. Even then I understood why my brother hit me. He needed to release his frustrations. It seemed like I was more emotionally stable than any one else with dad gone. Here I was as a young teenager taking on the responsibilities of caring for my mom, Elie, and Roger.

Roger was seven then. The school he attended was open, off and on, based on the status of the war. I tried to get him to do his homework, but I couldn't help him. It broke my heart that he too was having difficulty in school. I tried to pass on the lessons dad gave to me though. We all tried to protect Roger from the problems we were facing as a family, and I did my best to be there for him.

Attending school was out of the question for me. I was so behind that there was little chance that I'd ever catch up, especially with the learning disabilities I was facing. At thirteen, I had only made it to the fourth grade and I stuck out like a sore thumb. Most of my classmates were several years younger and a foot shorter, and my body was rapidly looking like a woman's.

It was difficult trying to be strong for everyone else. I needed someone to be strong for me. But I had no time to dwell on my grief. Life still had to go on. I had to roll up my sleeves and get to work. I washed the dishes, the laundry, and did the little bit of cooking I knew how to do. Having to do everything myself made me miss and appreciate all the hard work our former nanny Emgalal did.

*   *   *

Elie and the other young men in the area served as guards, looking out for signs of trouble. They carried guns and surrounded the neighborhood to protect it. Despite how poorly he treated me, I would worry about Elie when he was playing watchman. I didn't want to lose another brother.

"Don't go, Elie!" I begged him.

"I have to go," he said, strapping the gun across his chest. "I have to protect my family."

"No, please don't go, son," my mother begged and cried. As you know, Elie had always been one of her favorite sons and the thought of losing him was unbearable for her.

"Mother, I'm sorry, but I have to go. I love you." It was true. He did have to go. All the men were expected to protect the area.

One time, Elie was gone for several days. There had been lots of gunfire in the area and we were all worried that something had happened to him. We were so relieved and happy when he returned that we never even found out why he had been gone so long. Perhaps the responsibility of being the man of the house had become too much for him. Maybe he had to take a break and get away.

*   *   *

One day a huge battle broke out in the area where we were staying. With the threat of more bombings, a group of people loaded us onto a bus with many other families and we headed to a church in the mountains with the threat of bombing hanging over us the whole time. Due to limited space, we could only take bare necessities with us.

Within about two weeks, bombs were detonated in that region too. We were quickly moved out of the country to a large church in Syria, Lebanon's neighboring country. We slept in the main building and showered in the bathroom of the attached school. By that time, moving from place to place and sleeping on bare floors almost became routine. The local residents gave us whatever they could spare in food and clothing. Their generosity and church services kept us going and gave us *hope*.

I was about thirteen and a half and my body was maturing quickly. By that time, we were living in the church in Syria and there was one young Lebanese Armenian man who visited often. He loved to spend time with us and get to know other young Lebanese refugees. His name was Sevag. He was handsome and in his early twenties. Like us, he had lived in Lebanon and left to escape the war. Unlike us, Sevag was staying in a nice house with his older sister who was married to a rich and powerful man from Damascus, the capital of Syria. My family was living in the church, which made me feel uncomfortable with him because we had two completely different lifestyles. His family was doing well financially while mine was struggling.

Sevag made an extra effort to come to church so he could see me. Sometimes I would be flirtatious and romantic with him, but other times I would get scared and push him away. I was too young and wasn't ready for a relationship. It seemed like the more I pushed him away, the harder he would try to win my affections.

Back then, dating was viewed as a taboo. As teenagers, we'd talk about dating among ourselves, but we could never talk about it openly around adults. It was simply going out acting as if you were only friends. It was the custom then for young girls to not to go out with her friends for any reason without the company of at least one of her family members or another trusted adult. Especially as young as we were, it was important to be chaperoned.

Sevag would constantly ask me to go out with him. With his charming voice, he would say, "I want to spend time with you. How about we go to the movie, dinner, or whatever you want?" My friends who were living at the church with us were having fun seeing Sevag in love. They would say, "Aimmee, he's handsome, polite, and he loves you. You should give him a chance. Go have fun." Eventually I did, with Elie and Sevag's sister Kani accompanying us.

*   *   *

Within a few months, my dad had been working and selling his inventions in Egypt when he tracked us down through some old family friends in Syria. Dad visited for a week and helped us move from the church to his friends' home in Syria. It was such a busy week with dad that I didn't even see Sevag.

While dad was there, he did his best to add a bit of comfort to our lives by taking us to restaurants and spending as much quality time with us as possible. It was very comforting for me to spend the short time that Dad had with us. He left us his address and gave us as much money as he could before he had to return to Egypt for work.

As grateful as we were for the shelter and food we received at church, we were very happy to stay with dad's friends. It was nice taking a private shower, getting a home cooked meal, and experiencing some of the comforts of home. Somehow, Sevag found me there and continued to try to get my attention.

After the bombing had stopped for a while, mom, Elie, Roger, and I returned to our apartment in Beirut. A few days later, I was visiting with a neighbor and we were talking in her living room. Suddenly, Roger rushed in. He was breathing hard and could barely get any words out. "Roger, calm down. What's wrong?" I asked.

He replied, "Aimmee, guess who's here! Guess who's here!"

"Who?" I replied.

"Sevag," he excitedly said, "and he wants to see you!"

CHAPTER EIGHT

Getting Married at 14

I was so flattered when I heard Sevag had tracked me down from Syria.

"Oh wow," I said to myself.

Even though I was excited, I still didn't know what to say or do once I saw him. Everything I had ever been happy about in the past had been taken away.

"I came all the way here to ask for your hand in marriage," he said. "I love you so much and can't imagine myself living without you. I want to marry you." Sevag was in love and completely determined to make me his wife.

Even though I was young, mom thought the marriage was a great idea. After all, he came from a good family and was a skilled jeweler.

"Sevag would be a good husband, Aimmee," mom said. "He loves you and cares about you. What more could you ask for? I am sure he will take care of you. He's also handsome and polite. And let's face it. Right now, our family is really struggling financially."

Back then, most women didn't have many career opportunities so they followed the traditional path of becoming a wife and mother. Mom believed that getting married to Sevag would improve my status in life, since going back to school was no longer a realistic option for me.

Another reason it seemed that my mom wanted me to get married was so she wouldn't have to worry about me any longer. She knew she couldn't be there to give me the kind of advice and attention a teenage girl needs. Even before the war, Mom was detached and unavailable. By now, she was far worse. She had lost a son, was in the midst of a difficult financial situation, and was dealing with our family being physically separated and emotionally torn apart.

It was the tradition back then for a prospective groom's family to ask the bride's father for her hand in marriage. The families would discuss the matter and a marriage would take place only if both families agreed. Since my dad was out of the country seeking work, my mother was responsible for fulfilling his role. Regardless of her intentions, she was not in a position to make a sound decision. She had little common sense to begin with and on top of that, she was still grieving. With the heavy medication she was taking, mom practically became a different person. She grew dependent on the pills and our family had to deal with her drastic mood swings. Perhaps she was taking the wrong medication. Who knows? How was she supposed to be able to decide something as serious as whether or not to let her daughter, who was not yet fourteen, get married?

With dad and Jacque out of the country and Robert gone, Elie was the man of the house and therefore had a say in the matter. He had always been a mama's boy and refused to question our mother's decision. Although he was hurt that mom had never spent enough time with us when we were younger, he had a need to put her on a pedestal. He always wanted to please her, so he did not dispute the marriage.

When my mother asked Sevag to bring his family to ask for my hand in marriage, he was quick with an reasonable answer. He explained that they were still in Syria with his sister, Serune, who was very ill. He wanted to marry me before Serune died, so that we wouldn't have to wait a year or two. (The custom back then was that a family would not allow any type of celebration, like engagements or marriages, for a long time following the death of a family member.) He said he couldn't wait that long to have me as his wife. With his earnest displays of affection for me, Sevag had won over my mom. She soon started pressuring me to marry him. As young as I was, not quite fourteen, I started to believe that getting married was a good idea.

"Maybe everything would get better if I got married," I told myself. *"At least I wouldn't have to worry about Elie anymore. One day, I'd have children of my own and could be the kind of mother I had always wanted. What isn't there to like about Sevag? He's a nice smart guy,"* I thought. He also seemed to be crazy about me.

I had no idea what marriage was all about. Who would know anything about it at fourteen? Most people don't have a clue about it even at twice that age. My mind was taken off the war as I daydreamed about wearing a white dress and having a beautiful wedding.

In my dream world, Sevag would be my knight in shining armor. He would take care of me and rescue me from my family responsibilities. We'd have beautiful children, grow old together, and live happily ever after. Despite witnessing my parents' troubled marriage throughout my life, I was young and optimistic. I was eagerly buying in to all the bridal fantasies that most girls dream about.

In Lebanon, you have to be at least eighteen to get married without parental consent. After my mom convinced me that marrying Sevag was the right thing to do, I went along with her to sign the marriage papers. Even while we were walking down to the courthouse, I wavered back and forth in my mind, questioning whether what we were about to do was a good decision. I wanted to trust my mom, so I went along with the plan. I always had trouble writing, but that day, I had an especially hard time signing my name on the dotted line. Maybe that's because I didn't have that happy, giddy feeling expected of a young girl about to get married. Instead my head hung heavy and I felt groggy, like I hadn't quite woken up yet.

As far as I knew, neither mom nor Sevag had made contact with my dad, so I wondered if he would agree with what we were doing. I didn't ask my mom about it. I figured she would do whatever she believed my dad would agree with. Believing that Sevag's family had approved of the marriage, we carried on and broke tradition by proceeding without my father's express permission.

Three days after my fourteenth birthday, on a cold winter day, I was married. Maral, the distant cousin I became close to soon after Robert died, was my maid of honor. Her brother was the best man.

Sevag gave me a small, white and gold ring. We made a wonderful couple. I wore a long, beautiful dress that we borrowed from a neighbor, along with a little veil. Sevag looked so handsome in his brown suit. About thirty neighbors and relatives attended the wedding.

We were married in a traditional Armenian Orthodox church. I didn't understand anything the priest said since the ceremony was conducted in Armenian, which I didn't learn to speak until years later.

It was awkward having Elie walk me down the aisle arm in arm. Before, he had only touched me when hitting me. My oldest brother Jacque was out of the country with my father and I truly missed both of them being there. My family was out of communication with my older sister Jacqueline so she didn't even know I was getting married. I felt my dad's absence and wished he would somehow magically appear to share the day with me.

Most of all, I thought about Robert. There I was on my wedding day having flashbacks of the most tragic day of my life. Robert had high hopes and expectations for me. He wanted me to go to college and always told me, "Aimmee, don't you even think about getting married before you're eighteen." Every time he said those words, it always put a smile on my face. Deep inside, I felt good and safe because I knew he was lovingly trying to protect me and was looking out for my best interest. He didn't want me to get married young. Yet here I was getting married at a very early age. Was I dishonoring my older brother that I loved so much by being a child bride?

I looked out into the crowd and saw my mother and Roger, who I started worrying about right then and there. Was I doing the right thing? Suddenly, I was overcome with the overwhelming feeling that perhaps getting married wasn't a good idea. All the fairy tale images that had clouded my mind for the past several weeks vanished. Sevag picked up on my nervousness and did everything he could to make me feel comfortable during the ceremony. Finally, it started to dawn on me what I was really getting into.

But it was too late. The vows were said and the time came for Sevag to kiss his bride. Throughout the whole wedding, he seemed happy and excited and made me believe he had married the girl of his dreams. The fact that no one from his family had attended our wedding didn't even bother him.

We had a small reception at an Armenian lounge. Everyone appeared to be having a good time, listening to the music and dancing.

For a second, my memory drifted to childhood and my love for dancing. When I was a little girl, my grandmother Esma would play the *derbecki* (a small, handheld drum). All of her neighbors would sit around in a circle and put me in the middle. I enjoyed watching their elderly faces light up as I danced for them. Dancing was one of the few things that brought me out of my shell. When I danced, I didn't feel shy.

It was the tradition for a bride to dance with all the male members of her family at her wedding. However, when the time came for me to dance, I was sad that I didn't get the opportunity to dance with my father, Jacque or Robert.

After we cut the cake, Sevag and I went to a hotel in the mountains for our honeymoon. I had no idea what to do as a virgin. No one told me what would be expected. Mom had never discussed marital intimacy with me and I hadn't reached the point where I was really curious about learning.

For three long days, we stayed in the hotel. I was very uncomfortable being intimate with Sevag. For almost the entire honeymoon, I cried either out of fear or confusion. I was shy and didn't feel comfortable being undressed in front of him. My body would tense up and make intimacy impossible. Yet, he was very gentle and understanding. He even cried with me despite his frustration. We departed the hotel without having consummated the marriage. I had done the unthinkable; I left my honeymoon still a virgin.

Soon after our three day honeymoon, Sevag and I returned to Beirut to stay at my mom's apartment until his family came back from Syria. I was shocked to learn that Sevag's family had returned to Beirut, and had been living there even before he had come to ask my mom for my hand in marriage. He hadn't come all that way to find me like he said he had.

Sevag not only lied to my mother and me, but he also lied to his family. He knew that they would have disapproved of the marriage since we were both so young and because I came from a less fortunate family. He had never told them about his plans to get married or asked them to visit us to ask for my hand in marriage. Although Sevag's family had wanted him to marry a rich girl, and even had someone in mind for him when he was ready, he was going to force me on them.

In Middle Eastern culture, especially back then, children typically got married in order of age, starting with the oldest first. They wouldn't leave their parents' home until they did. Even if they were forty years old, they lived with their parents until their wedding day. If they didn't get married, they never left. Sevag knew that would be another reason his family would have disapproved of our marriage.

Sevag's older brother was named Hagob. He was still unmarried and living at home with his parents. When he found out that his younger brother had gotten married, he was completely surprised. Hagob located where we were living and came to talk to us. When we came downstairs from my mom's apartment to greet him face to face, Hagob's surprise turned into shock. To this day, I can see the expression on his face. He couldn't believe that Sevag had eloped while he was still so young. However, he had to accept it and he was grateful that his younger brother was still alive.

He took us to their mother's house, which was located on the top floor of a six story building in a nicer neighborhood. I had to wait at a neighbor's house while Sevag and Hagob went upstairs to tell their mother the news about our marriage.

The whole house was filled with extended family and neighbors. For a while, they had been acting as a volunteer search and rescue squad, supporting the family's efforts to find their missing son. Everyone had been worried sick. When everyone found out that he was back, throughout the building you could hear the crying and chatter caused by their mixed emotions.

The front door was wide open when I walked in. Everyone stared at me with their jaws dropped as if I were an alien. You can easily imagine how nervous and uncomfortable I was. Bad vibrations were everywhere and I immediately felt like an outsider. No one in the family seemed to want me there. I was so glad that Maral, my maid of honor, was with me. Besides Sevag and Hagob, she was the only one not looking at me like I was from outer space. I could hear the whispers around the room, *"I'm so glad he's back! I cannot believe he got married. What happened to him? How did that girl talk him into getting married?"*

Sevag was standing in front of his mother Emhagob trying to calm her down. (In Middle Eastern culture, a mother gets her name by adding *Em*, which means *mother of*, before the name of her eldest son. Therefore, Emhagob means mother of Hagob). She was screaming, rocking back and forth and throwing her hands up in the air. Over and over, she cried out loud, "What did you do Sevag?! What did you do?!" For an hour or two, the entire family argued. I couldn't understand what they was saying when they were speaking to each other in Armenian. It was pretty obvious that they were all angry at him. He had gone behind their backs to get married. There was nothing they could do about it. They had to accept it and move on, at least in that moment, to save face with the neighbors. They were embarrassed that they had been helping them look for him in earnest, only to find out that he was alive and well, having just eloped with some girl who they hadn't even met.

As word spread throughout the apartment building, more people came up to the house. Everyone wanted to see who the mystery girl was. One by one they entered, looking at me in amazement as if they had just seen a ghost.

All I could think about was the fact that I was stuck in this situation and there was nothing I could do. I knew that I was a kid without a voice, who had no strong family to back me up or protect me.

Deep in my heart, I wanted to tell everyone, *"Don't complain about what Sevag has done. Celebrate the fact that he's married and alive. Be happy for him. You don't know what it means to lose a loved one. Losing Robert taught me to appreciate life and each moment I have on this earth."*

I felt like I was fourteen going on forty. I took a deep breath and told myself, *"Okay Aimmee, in order to keep peace in your heart and mind, you need to look at things from a different perspective. I need to focus on the positive and on the lessons I can learn from this."* To keep my focus away from my circumstances, I started asking myself, *"What I am going to learn from this situation? What can I do to make things better?"* Those questions were endlessly wandering in my mind. I was determined to find a solution.

After things started to settle down, the family ordered us to dress in our wedding attire so they could have a party. They wanted to treat the neighbors to a feast and festivities to express their gratitude for their help and support.

The day after the party, I woke up feeling as if I were still dreaming. I was living in a new home with unfamiliar faces. A few moments later, reality sank in when my mother-in-law and Kani came in my room and said, "Come on! Get up! It's time for you to clean the mess from yesterday. Then, come to the kitchen and help us prepare breakfast." After cleaning, I set out the dishes and silverware for the meal. Suddenly, in a rude voice, Kani said, "Get in here. Take these plates of food and set them out on the table." I had to serve the whole family, which was very large. It included Sevag's grandfather, father, mother, his brother Hagob, his sisters living there, and of course, Sevag himself. They ate out on the balcony, chatting in Armenian, which I still could not understand. They didn't acknowledge me or invite me to eat with them.

I'll never forget the rejection and hurt I felt at that moment. I wasn't even given enough respect to be invited to eat with my husband. Just days after our wedding, I was shocked that he didn't insist that I sit down and have breakfast with him.

Holding back my tears, I sneaked away to the kitchen. I was getting ready to eat when Kani marched in and said, "You need to finish cleaning the plates first before you eat your breakfast." With that, she walked out.

Meanwhile, Sevag was enjoying his meal and basically ignored me. He was happy that his family seemed to forgive him for eloping.

While I was cleaning, Sevag's sister Serune, who was very ill, invited me to get something to eat. She had finished her breakfast and was sitting on the living room sofa. "Sit down next to me and take a break," she said. "I like you and I'm glad you're here." It felt so good hearing her say those words. She seemed to feel bad and even embarrassed by the way her family had been treating me. Apparently, she wanted to make up for their mistreatment and rudeness with her kindness.

It was easy to see that Serune had peace in her heart and mind. The few minutes I spent sitting with her were the first time I could catch my breath since I had arrived. She had something unique and special about her. It didn't take too long before I realized that she was able to keep her peace because she *wasn't* judging me. That was a powerful lesson I learned and applied throughout the years. I felt like she was an angel from above guiding me.

*   *   *

Later that day, my mother-in-law Emhagob asked for proof that I was a virgin. Back then a girl was expected to be a virgin when she got married. After the honeymoon, it was custom to provide proof of her virginity to her in-laws. A girl usually bleeds following her first sexual experience. This blood is placed onto a white cloth and presented to the husband's family. If she didn't bleed and her husband was expecting her to do so since he had not had sex with her yet, he could send his new bride back to her family without cause. If that happened, she would have been considered a disgrace and essentially would be looked down upon for the rest of her life. Good thing I had nothing to worry about.

They didn't believe it when my husband uncomfortably explained that not only was I a virgin when we married, but that I was still a virgin because we still hadn't consummated the marriage. They thought I was lying about my age too, taking me for at least sixteen or seventeen. They seemed to be sure I wouldn't pass the virginity test and were banking on sending me back to my family, putting a quick end to what they felt was a family nightmare. I was already nervous about getting intimate with my husband and having the family rooting against my virginity made me altogether more uneasy. There was no way I could feel comfortable in that house full of people and bad vibes, so we needed somewhere else to go for the precious moment to occur. One of the neighbors offered to let us use their apartment, so we stayed for several days.

The same tradition requiring me to stain the white cloth also required my in-laws to present it to my family, along with a gift of appreciation for my virginity. Mom said that my mother-in-law was quite hasty and distant when she handed my mom a basket of chocolates and the blood-stained cloth that carried evidence of my first experience as a woman. "Here, your daughter is a virgin," she said without a smile, almost frowning as if she had just lost a big bet.

That ritual was supposed to be a happy occasion that would bring our families closer together. However, it was the first time my in-laws had visited mine. My father was still away. They were dismayed to discover that my family was struggling financially, which gave Kani and Sevag's mother another reason to look down on me. They were also disappointed that they couldn't send me back because I passed the virginity test.

They had to accept that I was there to stay, and decided to let Sevag and me live in one of the bedrooms in their house. My relationship with the family had already gotten off to a rough start and living with them only aggravated things. What made matters worse was that I didn't speak Armenian, so it was difficult not knowing what they were saying.

My in-laws' lifestyle was very different from the one I was used to. Like every family, they had their own particular rules and ways of doing things.

There I was living in a house with my husband and seven other people. I felt so out of place. I couldn't understand most of them and I knew that they were mad at me for marrying their son and brother. Of course I liked him, but I married him based on my mom's naïve recommendation. I wasn't ready for marriage or prepared to deal with the family struggles I was about to face.

*   *   *

Kani had been nice when she accompanied Sevag and me on several dates in Syria. However, she wasted no time trying to turn everyone against me. She would tell him that he was too young to be married and that he should be single and carefree. I often heard her say, "Our family is better off than hers. Don't you see that? She and her mom took advantage of you and tricked you into marrying her." Kani saw me as a weakling she could toy around with. Mistreating me became her game. She had a bullying personality and was the type of person who had to put someone else down to make herself feel good. She knew I didn't feel I had the right to speak up for myself, so she could get away with tormenting me. Who would have believed me anyway?

My mother-in-law was very emotional at the time, dealing with an ill daughter and trying to accept some strange new girl who came out of nowhere and married her son.

She was a true matriarch, a proud and somewhat domineering woman. She wanted the best for her family and made sure that they got it no matter what.

She had always been able to keep her kids out of trouble and get them to do things that she felt was in their best interest. That's why it really hurt her that her son had gone behind her back to get married. She would never have approved of the marriage and felt like her parental control had been undermined.

My husband soon started to act stand-offish with me when his family was around, in an attempt to please them. I could tell he still had feelings for me, yet Kani was slowly but steadily brainwashing him into believing he had made a mistake. He spent most of his time ignoring me, except when he wanted to be intimate.

Even though the problems I had with my mother-in-law, Kani and Sevag, the rest of the family treated me kindly. Their father and grandfather didn't speak to me much, as they were both quiet, reserved types, but they were nice to me when they did. I especially liked Sevag's older brother, Hagob, who treated me like I was his little sister. I looked up to Hagob, who reminded me a lot of Robert.

Kani couldn't treat me as poorly as she wanted to when Hagob was around. She knew he would defend me. He had even put his foot down when Kani and my mother-in-law were talking about sending me back to my family before I passed the virginity test.

When I first met my sister-in-law Mary, with her greenish-blue eyes and light brown waist-long hair that would shine golden in the sunlight, I thought I had met an angel. She was the youngest sister, who would often ask me to enjoy a tea break with her. Mary spent most of her time at home doing school work. Like most thirteen year olds, she was still a student. I was always worried that she'd ask me to help her with her homework and would discover that I couldn't read very well. I kept this fact well hidden from the whole family. I was good at doing that and had learned how to live in my shell. Mary and I were very close in age, but our lives were completely different.

Mary and Serune had similar spirits. They both were peaceful and kind-hearted. However, unlike Mary, Serune was sick. Her skin was pale and her body frail. Yet, from within her radiated a great inner beauty. There appeared to be a halo around her that made the room she was in brighter. No matter what she was going through, every time she saw me, she opened her arms, welcoming me with love and a big smile on her face. I was grateful to have her in my life. Being around her taught me many insightful lessons . . .

CHAPTER NINE

My New Home

Several weeks after my wedding, Serune became increasingly weak as her health rapidly declined. Her light was beginning to fade. She had been ill for a long time. The stress of war did not make it easier on her health. As the family were preparing to take her to the hospital, she looked at me with her beautiful big eyes and whispered, "I am going to be okay." Sadly, that was the day when she lost her battle to the illness. Everyone began mourning.

Serune had always made a special effort to make me feel comfortable. Although I only knew her for a little while, we had become close friends quickly. I was devastated and sad to see her leave this world so young. She was only in her twenties. Every time she said good morning and good evening, it made my heart smile. Each second I spent with her was incredibly valuable. How she lived her life taught me how important it is not to judge.

On that sad day, I saw light *through* the darkness. I learned something powerful. *We don't have a choice of when it's time for us to leave, but we do have a choice of what we leave behind.* Her light had been contagious. I was determined to keep peace in my heart and to be an example to others, just like her. I promised myself that no matter what happened, I would do my best not to judge.

In Lebanon, the deceased are cleaned up at the hospital and then brought back home. For a day or two, the family can pay their last respects and say goodbye. If the departed is an unmarried female, she is dressed up in a wedding gown. As Serune was laid on the bed in the living room, she looked like an angelic sleeping bride.

When they came to pick her up, she was placed into her casket and carried out of the building. Before putting her in the hearse, the pallbearers made her casket dance in the air, symbolic of the bridal dance she would never perform.

For forty days and forty nights, the house was filled with family and friends dressed in black who did nothing but cry and mourn. We could not turn on the television or listen to the radio. No weddings, no engagements, no Christmas trees. Only mourning.

Even neighbors were expected to respect a grieving family. Although they continued to live their lives, they would tone down or refrain from holding any kind of celebration around a mourning family.

Serune's burial site was visible off in the distance from my mother-in-law's balcony, where she would sit crying from sun up to sundown. She'd look out toward the cemetery, talking non-stop in a chant-like fashion to her deceased daughter. *"Where did you go, Serune? Why did you leave me?"*

Despite how my mother-in-law had treated me up to that point, my heart grieved for her. I felt her pain, but I wasn't in a position to say anything. She didn't want to get to know me, so I didn't push myself on her. I knew how it felt to lose a loved one and realized that she was going through a lot. To keep peace in my heart, I followed Serune's example and made a decision not to judge her.

Even after the forty days had passed, everyone was still depressed and mourning. Sevag's father started drinking heavily to help him cope with his daughter's death and his emotional wife. All day long he would watch TV, drink *arak* (a popular local spirit), smoke cigarettes and maybe eat a little *mazze* (a snack to go with an alcoholic drink). He was a man of few words before Serune's death. After she died, he hardly spoke at all.

Hagob and Mary's kindness kept me going and helped me to cope with my day-to-day life. They let me take breaks and catch my breath between run-ins with Kani, dealing with my mother-in-law's depression, and my distant spouse Sevag.

I lived in their house feeling invisible and alone. I couldn't go anywhere, not even down the street, without permission from my husband or mother-in-law. When I asked for permission to go spend the day with my family, they seemed shocked. "Why would you want to go spend the day in that small apartment in such an old building?" they would ask. It was if I had insulted them with my request.

Living with my in-laws was very hard. Kani was constantly trying to convince both my mother-in-law and my husband that I was some sort of monster. It was three against one. Standing up for myself was impossible. I felt crushed and defeated.

*　　*　　*

One day, my mom came for a visit. My mother-in-law rudely greeted her at the door and coldly led her to the living room to sit down. Kani was standing in front of the bathroom, barking orders and telling me what to clean next. When I heard my mother's voice, I instantly became happy and started to get up. She stopped me and said, "Keep cleaning. You cannot visit with your mom until you're finished. If you want to see her, you better hurry." She pointed at the remaining dirty spots and said, "You still need to finish here and there." I started crying.

"Please, please let me say hello to my mother, Kani," I begged with tears streaming down my face."

"No! Not until you're done," she snapped, blocking me from leaving. She had this smug grin on her face and a look in her eyes that dared me to defy her.

Mom overheard the conversation and could see what Kani was doing. However, there was nothing she could do to stop it. Since mom didn't know how to handle this situation, she quickly picked up her purse and left. The mistreatment I was experiencing hurt my mother so bad, that to this day she still remembers the incident. She says she'll take that memory to her grave.

Unfortunately, my mom was not strong enough to stand up for me and defend me. She felt she had no right to say anything in that house and felt guilty due to allowing me to get married without my in-laws' or father's approval. Had she adhered to tradition, the marriage would never have happened because Sevag's family would not have agreed. Therefore, I would not have endured the mistreatment and disrespect she had witnessed that day. Her decision forced me to enter Sevag's house without the respect a bride typically receives from her in-laws. Since they had never agreed to accept me as part of their family, I received no honor in their house. Kani, in particular, made it clear that I was an unwelcome outsider.

In order to keep hope and peace in my heart, I had to use all the wisdom I had learned. I kept telling myself, *"Don't judge Aimmee. Don't judge. They don't know you. One day, they will get to know you and everything will change."*

* * *

About two months into my marriage, my father came back from his travels. I was so excited to learn about his return that I started jumping up and down. My mother-in-law and Kani couldn't understand why I was so thrilled and happy. I explained that I loved my father very much and that I hadn't seen him in a long time. I couldn't wait to spend time with him.

My mother-in-law responded, "Well, you will see him when we give you permission." I stood there for a second not believing what she said. I felt like someone had sucked the life out of me.

Disheartened, I went to my room and closed the door. Both windows were open and the air pressure made the door shut hard and fast, as if I had slammed it.

From my room, I could hear the family speaking Armenian, but I didn't know what they were saying. A few moments later, Sevag came into the room, and asked, "Why did you slam your door?"

"The window was open and made the door close like that," I told him. "I didn't intentionally slam it shut."

"Go apologize to my mother and kiss her hand for slamming the door like that!" he ordered, raising his voice.

His statement confused me. "Why should I have to apologize for something I didn't do?" I asked.

He began yelling and told me, "You must do it now!"

It hit me that my relationship with Sevag was going to be like my parents' marriage, with lots of arguing and yelling. It was something that I wasn't expecting. There I was, newly married, and already fighting with my husband about something that I didn't do. It made me deeply sad that I had to live that kind of life.

"If you want to see your father, you will have to go and kiss my mother's hand right now!" he screamed.

I swallowed my pride. Entering the living room with tears streaming down my face, I fell on my hands and knees before my mother-in-law. I felt so small at that moment, but I wanted to visit my dad and was willing to do anything. They were playing a cruel game. I told myself, *"Stop crying Aimmee and just do what you have to do. If I do it, I win. I'll get to see my dad."* I knew I couldn't control or influence how the family treated me. The only thing I could do was be in control of my thoughts and emotions.

When I took her hand to kiss it, my mother-in-law pushed me away and started speaking Armenian. I didn't know what she was saying, but I knew she was angry. Everyone else started talking among themselves. I was so confused. All I wanted was to see my father.

Sevag's older brother Hagob jumped up and started yelling at the family. Even though I didn't understand what he was saying, I knew he was coming to my defense.

"Get ready, Aimmee! I'm going to take you to see your father right now," he said.

I was crying and happy at the same time. Hagob took Sevag and me to see my father. During the drive over, Hagob asked me not to tell my dad about what had happened. I willingly agreed.

When my father opened the door, he immediately noticed that I had been crying. He could see my red and swollen eyes.

"Why are you crying?" dad inquired, with a concerned look on his face.

"I'm just happy to see you," I said.

As dad and I started catching up, I could see the disappoinment on his face concerning mom's decision to approve my marriage. I was surprised to discover that Sevag had written to my father while he was in Egypt and asked for my hand in marriage. My dad had written back saying, "My daughter still needs her mother's milk. When she is older, you can talk to me about marrying her." I realized then that he had knowingly ignored and overruled my father's wishes.

*   *   *

When I finished my daily chores or when no one else was around, I would hide away in my room and try to improve my reading ability. Even though I couldn't read long passages, I enjoyed reading the love stories in *Rima*, an Arabic magazine. It was filled with pictures and only had a small amount of text, which was not overwhelming. It gave me the opportunity, little by little, to improve my reading.

I'd get lost in the stories and sometimes my mother-in-law would catch me reading them. "Why do you need love stories?" she'd ask, "You're already married. Those stories are for young, unmarried girls."

Along with becoming a better reader, I was also starting to speak and understand Armenian well. This helped me get a good sense of how things worked in my in-laws' house.

Kani was a manipulative strategist. She always liked to control everything and knew how to manipulate the entire family. Her overbearing and talkative personality helped her get her way with anything and everything. The fact that she was absolutely gorgeous also played to her advantage.

Even though everyone underestimated me and viewed me as a naïve young teenager, I was able to recognize what Kani was doing. I refused to play her games. Every time she pushed me to a breaking point, I would just simply walk away. Despite always being weak in school, I was very perceptive for a young girl and picked up on things that most adults missed. (Decades later, the whole family got a taste of who Kani truly was and began to see what she was capable of doing).

Seeing things in a different perspective had always been a gift. I kept telling myself that it was a skill that I could not neglect. However, doubts and fears would constantly sneak into my heart like a thief. Even at a young age, I clearly understood that it was *my responsibility* to constantly protect my heart and put my gift to use.

*　　*　　*

My mother-in-law didn't accept me. On the other hand, she kept pressuring me to get pregnant. "Are you ever going to have a baby?" she'd ask. So every month when I got my period, I was so disappointed. I felt like something was wrong with me. In those days, wives were expected to immediately bear children. Women could not delay, and not having children was not an option.

About five months into the marriage, I finally got pregnant. When I was about six months along, Hagob, Kani, and some friends had a small party at our house. Every
one was having fun that night, including me for a change. They were enjoying themselves so much, that after the party, they wanted to drive to the mountain and continue. I wanted to go with them. However, Sevag already had enough to drink and I was expected to clean up after everyone. We ended up staying home. I was disappointed we weren't going. You can imagine a fifteen year old just starting to have fun and then being told to stop. Sevag went to sleep and I went to work. I cleaned as much as I could and later went to bed.

I was abruptly woken up early in the morning by crying and screaming. I discovered that our house was filled with neighbors and families. For a few moments, I was in denial of what was going on. I couldn't believe it and kept thinking, *"No, no, this isn't happening. I'm dreaming right now."* Unfortunately, it was not a dream and I had to accept the horrible news. On his way back from the party, Hagob had a deadly accident. Despite how my mother-in-law treated me, it was hard for me to see her in pain. In my opinion, the most painful thing in life is losing someone you care about. I know that feeling very well. By that time, I had lost five people close to me: my grandma, Robert, my grandpa, Serune, and now Hagob.

Thoughts started filling my mind, *"If we had gone with Hagob . . . If I was with him in the car . . . he probably wouldn't have driven so fast knowing I'm pregnant. He would probably still be alive right now if we had gone. Or maybe we'd all be dead. Maybe by not going the baby's life was saved."* On that day, I accepted that there is a *reason* for everything in this life. This perspective helped me look at the situation and release the guilt.

Hagob was buried next to his sister Serune. My mother-in-law had already been grieving for her. Now with two children gone, she mourned almost non-stop as she looked out toward the cemetery from the balcony.

I deeply missed Hagob and I felt a void in my life. As the oldest son, Hagob was the only family member with authority who treated me with respect. I remembered his kindness, and how he was the only family member to give me a Christmas present. More importantly, he made me feel welcomed and loved.

Getting married and having a baby are supposed to be joyous occasions. Yet during both my newlywed season and pregnancy, I was wearing black, mourning the death of someone close. I was only fifteen, an age when most girls were still in school frolicking about without a care in the world. My life was so different from theirs.

I was already treated poorly before Hagob died. After his death, I was treated even worse. I received little respect before, and afterwards I got none. My mother-in-law and Kani only spoke to me when giving orders. I felt all alone due to the almost non-existent relationship with my husband. We couldn't talk about anything.

Seeing Roger or the rest of my family was rare. I continued to be the family maid, being forced to clean after everyone. Meanwhile, I was getting heavy with child and becoming increasingly emotionally and physically exhausted. Through it all, the war raged on . . .

CHAPTER TEN

Motherhood at 15

A month after we lost Hagob in a tragic car accident, the war was getting worse. Militias were fighting against each other. Christian against Christian, Muslim against Muslim, Muslim, against Christian. For a while we didn't know who was fighting against whom.

For several days there had been consistent bombing in the area. One night, the bombing got really bad and the residents of the building gathered together on the lower floors, where it was safer. We had no electricity and it was total chaos. We didn't know if we'd live to see another day. Every time I heard a bomb drop, I began to shiver and my heart started pounding. All of a sudden, I felt something weird happening in my body. An old, wise neighbor looked at me and asked, "What's happening Aimmee? What's wrong? Are you OK?" Hiding my contractions was *not* an option. My child was determined to enter the world two months ahead of schedule. Perhaps fear broke my water.

Within minutes, I was in the backseat of a car. Sevag and Kani's fiancée John, were taking me to the hospital. They were speeding all the way there. Holding myself tightly, I was caught in between pain and fear. Left and right, bombs were dropping. It looked like we were in the middle of a fire storm. We went to the first and closest hospital we could think of. When we got there safely, I took a deep breath of relief.

The nurses were busy serving their numerous patients. The three of us stood there in shock when a nurse ran up to us and said, "Go home and give birth there. We don't have any room for you." Disappointed and afraid, we left that hospital only to be denied by several others. A couple of hospitals suggested that we find a midwife. After a long search, we finally found a birthing center willing to take us in.

It was a long and exhausting birth. As I was looking around, I could hear and see everyone panicking. The baby kept moving upward, making me short of breath. Two nurses had to press down on my belly to help me push her out. I could see the fear in their eyes as they both kept screaming, "Push! Push!" I was only fifteen and this was my first birth. Naturally, I was confused and scared. I was in so much pain that even Sevag cried for me. That was one of the few times I felt close to him. Just minutes after the delivery, I fell asleep from exhaustion. I knew I had given birth to a girl, but I couldn't keep my eyes open.

From the first time I laid my eyes on her and held her in my arms, I felt a special connection and love that I cannot explain. For three days, baby Silva was kept in an incubator. When I took her home, she was very ill. She was very skinny and couldn't keep food down. Whenever I fed her, she would throw up, turning the skin on her neck red and making it peel from all the acid coming up.

My mother and grandmother thought the problem was that I was just inexperienced with babies, so they took Silva for a few days, which gave me a much needed break. But caring for Silva was too much even for them, so my break came to an abrupt end.

*   *   *

Every mother in the world loves hearing that her child is the most beautiful and healthy child ever. Yet at times, my mother-in-law would help me give Silva a shower and say, "Is this the best you can give me for a grandchild? Look at her. She looks like a chicken. She's so small and skinny." Her comments made me feel inferior. I felt like no matter what I did, it was never good enough.

We took Silva to many doctors, but none of them knew what to do for her. All they could tell us was that she'd probably get better when she was a year old, after her immune system was fully developed. One day, we had to rush her to the hospital and discovered that she was extremely dehydrated. She needed an IV but her body was very tiny. After trying unsuccessfully for hours, they had no choice but to slit her wrist and leg to find a vein. Almost three decades later, she still wears scars from those cuts.

Soon after Silva was born, I promised her that I would do everything in my power to give her a better life than I had. I wanted to give her everything I wanted but couldn't have as a child: attention, a stay-at-home mother who'd shower her with love and affection, and a stable, happy household. I was willing to pay any price to keep our family together for her.

Lebanese culture is based on family values and traditions, and I wanted Silva to hold her head up high, secure in the knowledge that she came from an intact home. I would picture her as a young woman and that we would be best friends. With Silva, I finally had my own flesh and blood and someone on my team. She was mine and no one could take her away from me.

When I got married, I was not welcomed and treated like a new bride should have been. Similarly, motherhood didn't bring with it the attention a new mom would normally receive according to Lebanese custom either. After giving birth, our custom is that a woman is pampered for forty days so her body has time to recover. Yet when my daughter was born, everyone was still mourning her Aunt Serune and Uncle Hagob, so she received no presents welcoming her into the world. I had no recovery time at the house. While I was at the hospital, they didn't do any cleaning. When I got back, I was still expected to do all the household chores. On top of that, I had to take care of my daughter's health needs. I was swamped and drowning in responsibilities, desperately needing help, yet nobody reached out.

Silva usually slept during the day and stayed awake all night. When she was suffering from abdominal pain, she would keep the family and the neighbors awake with her loud crying. I did everything possible to make her feel better. Regardless of giving it my best effort with every idea I could think of, it didn't work. This just made me feel worse as a mother.

The responsibilities assigned to me by the family took most of the day. Since I wasn't getting any disposable diapers, I was up late three or four nights a week washing Silva's cloth diapers, along with the rest of the laundry. By the next day, I was always exhausted. Getting little to no sleep made doing the daily housework twice as difficult. Hanging cloth diapers out to dry on our sixth floor balcony was hard, especially during windy and cold winter nights. I appreciated every time I was able to use a disposable diaper.

Even with all the challenges, holding my daughter in my arms, close to my heart, helped me endure every ounce of struggle. She was my *why*, my reason for living. She kept me moving forward. Whenever I felt overwhelmed and empty, I would hurry to her to hold her close to my heart. When we discover and know our why in life, we are able to keep going no matter what the situation may be.

Around that time, one of my uncles, my father's older brother Karim, was shot by a sniper as he crossed a bridge and was left to die. We had stayed with Uncle Karim for several weeks after losing everything to the bomb that killed Robert. It was a lot for my father to handle and was sad to lose another family member who had helped us in a time of need.

*   *   *

Kani had taken over the two clothing stores that Silva's uncle Hagob owned and operated before he died. Sevag helped a little, but most of the time he sat outside flirting with girls passing by. One day, I decided to take Silva to see her dad at the family clothing store. It was the first time I had left the house without permission. I was almost sixteen and had been working up the courage to assert myself as a woman capable of leaving the house by herself and returning safely. I just wanted to be like everyone else. I took a taxi to the store and hoped that he would be happy to see us.

"I came to say hello and bring Silva to see you," I told him, watching the look of surprise on his face quickly fade into anger.

"You have no business here," he snarled.

I let his comment go and started looking at the clothes.

"What do you think you're doing? Don't even think about it. You're not getting anything. Take your daughter and go back home!" he yelled. "Who gave you permission to leave the house anyway?"

"I thought you might want to see Silva," I said with disappointment. All I wanted was a taste of freedom. I didn't want to start an argument.

"You have to ask before you leave the house!" he replied.

He had this way of making me feel like I was beneath him. I never learned why he was so angry to see me.

I knew he cheated on me and in my heart I was deeply hurt and disappointed. I didn't feel I was good enough or that I had a right to expect a great marriage. I wasn't special, so I just blindly accepted his actions. I told myself, *"I have better things to worry about than what he is doing."*

I felt like I was Kani's personal slave. When I tried to tell Sevag how she was treating me, he wouldn't listen. I wanted us to move to get away from the mistreatment I got from Kani and his mother. My hope was for us to stand on our own two feet.

"You're my husband. I'd appreciate it if you would make a living and support us. I can't handle being a slave to your sister any longer," I told him one day.

He snapped back, "Shut up! If it weren't for my sister, we wouldn't be able to make it! I never want to hear you say that again! Do you understand?"

I had no choice to obey his requests and move on.

* * *

I used to love it when my brother Elie would come to visit. Despite the years of his physically abusing me, what I went through with Eile was nothing compared to what I was going through at that time. Having a member of my own family close by was a welcome break from my life as Kani's personal servant.

Sevag became a different man while Elie was there. His attitude toward me would completely change. He acted like a good, loving husband. Even though I knew it wasn't sincere, at that point I would take anything that would lift my spirit, even if it only lasted a few hours.

Sometimes my little brother Roger would walk the long way from my parents' house to visit me. My mother-in-law would see him in the distance from the balcony.

"Aimmee, your brother is coming," she would say. By that time, I was speaking Armenian fairly well and could understand what she was saying.

"What are you doing walking out here by yourself?" I asked Roger. "What if the bombs were to start striking?"

"I missed you and wanted to come see you. I was lonely. Mom's not at home," he told me, which broke my heart.

Our mother was in Saudi Arabia during that time. Shortly after I got married, she went there to visit my older brother Jacque and ended up staying. She said she couldn't handle coming back to Lebanon to face the war, so she found a job and stayed at Jacque's house.

I would worry about Roger and wonder who was taking care of him with my mother gone. My father was in Lebanon, but he was having heart problems and also trying to make a living. Elie was a young man with a life of his own, so he wasn't willing to stay home to take care of his little brother. He wanted to go out and have fun.

Along with not being allowed to visit my family's home as often as I would have liked, I was exhausted from raising Silva and doing all the household chores. In reality, I didn't have any extra time to take care of my little brother anyway. I felt helpless and sad that I couldn't do anything for him. Every night when I went to bed, I spoke to my imaginary best friend and asked God for guidance.

* * *

Kani and Sevag liked to go out on Saturday nights. "Get dressed Aimmee. We're going out. Be ready to leave soon," Saveg would say. The tone of his voice always sounded mean and unenthusiastic. It felt as if I were a burden and they had to take me with them. I couldn't even ask what we were going to do. They wouldn't give me the chance to decide whether or not I wanted to go. Having an opinion was not an option. As much as I wanted to go out like any normal teenager, how they treated me squashed my excitement and ruined the fun. I felt like a prisoner who was always given orders. I had no rights, no say and no choice. This was how things unfolded every time I was told we were going out.

One Saturday, we stopped by Kani's clothing store. Everyone, except for me, went inside to get something new to wear. Kani wouldn't let me go in, so I sat outside in the parked car looking through the window as she, Sevag, and their friends picked out new outfits. No one even acknowledged me or asked if I wanted anything. It was especially hurtful that my own husband wouldn't invite me inside.

Kani would also try on new clothes in front me. She'd bring a bagful or two of selections from the store and ask me to tell her what looked best on her. After she'd decide what she liked, she'd go through her old stuff and throw it on the floor. "You can have those," she'd say. I didn't mind wearing used clothes, but I felt sad that she was treating me this way only to hurt me on purpose. She thought she was tricking me, yet it was obvious to me that her intention was to build herself up and tear me down. Controlling was her thing to do. There is a huge difference between *controlling* and being *in control*. Fortunately I knew how to be in control which helped me to stay alert and centered. Finally, when she was finished teasing me, she would order me to get her coffee.

Most every Sunday, my in-laws would have a barbecue. They would be socializing and eating out on the balcony while I was stuck in the kitchen. It was an unpleasant feeling. Being alone always made me vulnerable to traumatic flashbacks of the bombing that took Robert's life. Inevitably, I'd end up breaking some dishes. This was a great source of entertainment for Kani and my mother-in-law, who would make fun of me.

"How does she think she could ever learn to cook when she can't even handle washing dishes?" they'd say.

They even started expecting me to break a dish or two. When I approached the sink to begin washing, I'd hear one of them ask the other, "How long do you think it'll take for her to drop one this time?"

Even though their snide remarks wreaked havoc on my self-esteem, causing me to believe that I really couldn't do something as simple as wash dishes correctly, I started to laugh with them, in an attempt to be friendly and get along. It was my way of trying to fit in and get close.

During meals, Sevag would sit at one end of the table and I had to sit on the opposite side, closest to the door. That way if anyone needed anything, I could be at their beck and call. I had to serve everyone, so I was always the last one to sit down to eat. I was also the first one to get up since I had to clean.

After each meal, the family would go sit in the living room and play cards, chess, or some other game. I was never invited to sit down and enjoy the fun.

One day, I decided to be courageous and asked, "Can I play too?"

Sevag shot back, saying, "You don't even know how to play. Go finish your work."

I could tell by the sarcastic looks on everyone's face that they agreed with him. I stood there in shock with my jaw on the ground. I had no idea what to say or do. I told myself, *"They don't think I know how to play, but here I am taking care of the house and raising a baby."* Disheartened by his rejection, I put my daughter in the stroller and took her into the kitchen with me. As I washed the dishes, I kept looking down at her sweet face. I felt she was my support system. A gift from God. She was my why that kept me going. That's the power of having a *why*.

*   *   *

When I got married, my teenage life was taken away. No matter how old, a married Lebanese woman was expected to act a certain way back then. Although I was just a teenager, I had to walk, talk, dress, and act like a thirty-year-old.

I remember once when Mary, Sevag's younger sister, let me try on some of her new clothes. They looked really nice on me, as they did on her.

"Take those off," my mother-in-law snapped at me as she walked by. "Those are for a girl, not a married woman."

"What's the big deal mom?" Mary asked. "Let her wear them."

"No, she doesn't need to wear them. They're your clothes," she responded.

Every time I walked out on the balcony, I was reminded of the life I didn't have. Standing there, I always watched girls my age walk down the street. They looked beautiful dressed in youthful clothing, and it seemed like they didn't have a care in the world. However, the truth always came back to me. I have a beautiful daughter. I may not have a life like theirs, but what I have is worth it. I always focused on what I had, which helped me overcome many of life's challenges.

*   *   *

During a particular visit to my parents' house, the bombing got really bad. Everyone in the apartment building went to seek shelter down in the basement, which stunk of mold and mildew from leaky pipes. About a hundred of us gathered around the approximately thousand-square-foot area that had no electricity or running water.

Fortunately, my dad had always planned for emergencies and kept a bucket of water down there, just in case something were to happen. Everyone used to tease him about being overly cautious. Now those same people were begging him for a sip of water.

If my dad hadn't put the water down there, I would not have been able to feed Silva. I was able to give her enough formula to keep her from starving. We all had to share the limited water supply. Despite that we ended up having to stay down in the basement for seven days while bombs dropped in the area.

During a lull in the activity, Elie went to our unit to catch a good nap. While he was there, the bombing started to pick up again. We sat in fear as we heard the explosions getting closer and closer. And then, suddenly, we were all jostled together as we felt one hit our building, bringing with it flashbacks of my brother, Robert's tragic death.

My mom, who was visiting from Saudi Arabia, immediately flew into a panic. She knew Elie was upstairs. "Where's Elie!? Where's Elie!?" she screamed in terror as she looked around the room. She had already lost one son to a bomb and sensed that she might have lost another. Just as she started to cry, the basement door flung wide open and Elie ran inside. He was heading downstairs just as the bomb hit, and barely escaped death by a matter of seconds.

Later, we found out that of all the units in the building, that bomb specifically hit ours. My parents' apartment was left in shambles and my family lost everything again. However, we were happy and thankful that Elie was safe and sound.

When the bombs would slow down, we'd sneak outside to catch a breath of fresh air. The sky was hazy from the smoke and the air was so thick that we felt it was better to go back down to the basement, which reeked of mildew and the stench of people who hadn't showered for several days.

We occasionally left the basement to quickly use the restrooms upstairs, fearing that bombs would stike and kill us. Once finished, we rapidly ran back down to safety and felt lucky we didn't die during something as simple as a bathroom break. As needed, the men would leave to find something for everyone to eat. Women did everything they could to support and comfort each other. In order to stay sane in a war situation, we had to keep ourselves healthy mentally, spiritually, and emotionally. It is crucial to have love, open communication and commitment to our families, friends and neighbors.

After the bombing subsided and the roads were opened again, Sevag came looking for us. He could see that my family's apartment had been hit by a bomb and thought that something happened to us. When he found us, he hugged us and cried, happy to discover that we were okay. That moment was another one of the few times I felt close to him. That experience taught us the same principal; *love is the main ingredient in the journey of life*. Unfortunately, he chose not to apply it.

*　　*　　*

Whenever we could, Sevag, Silva, and I would go to Damascus, Syria, along with the rest of his family, to get away from the war in Lebanon. We'd stay with his older sister who lived there.

One evening, we were invited for dinner at his sister's friend's house. Every one got dressed up, but I had nothing dressy to wear, so I got a little bit of clothing here and there from my sisters-in-law. Nothing fit properly though. The stockings were too loose and were falling down. The shoes were so big that when I walked up the stairs, they were slipping off in the back, hitting the steps, click-clacking behind me.

I was the only one wearing ill-fitting clothes and felt like Cinderella did when the clock struck midnight, returning her clothing to rags. Suddenly, I started to laugh about how I was dressed and the embarrassing click clacking noise from my shoes. (It's okay if you're snickering right now too!) Sometimes, the best thing to do is to simply let go of things and laugh.

*　　*　　*

I was sixteen years old when I found out that I was pregnant again. The family wanted me to have a boy so I could name him after their deceased son Hagob and carry on the family name. I also wanted a son. I thought that I might get a little more respect if I did. I prayed so hard that the baby would be a boy.

"You better pray for that Aimmee," my mother-in-law would say. "If you give birth to another girl, I'll drop her off of the sixth story balcony, so you better keep praying."

Silva was only around nine months old at the time and was still as sick as she was the first day she was born. I would wash her clothes and bathe her three or four times a day.

Housekeeping expectations in Lebanon are much higher than they are in the United States. Cleaning in my native country is very labor intensive. The houses have tile instead of carpet and the floor is expected to be mopped every day. Each week, we would beat the dust out of the rugs and put them back on the floor. Caring for Silva, cleaning for a large family, and being pregnant on top of that, I became so weak I could barely stand.

Kani didn't care though. She'd wait till I had just mopped the long hallway and then she'd walk all over it, leaving tracks behind. "Oh well, I guess you'll just have to do it again," she'd say as she cast me a wicked grin. I was already so tired and weak that I couldn't catch my breath. In order to keep myself sane and not get angry, I kept *focusing* on my daughter, my *why*. I continued telling myself, *"Now I am going to have another why. I have responsibilities. My daughter and the child I'm carrying are the most important things. I need to stay strong for them."*

Around that time, my dad's younger brother died. He was losing family members left and right. Uncle Garabet was his younger brother and his death was especially hard. I remember him stopping by a lot when I was a kid. I would look forward to his visits and enjoyed his company. I appreciated the time he spent talking to me. He would give me advice, explaining right from wrong. After he died, I missed him dearly. His memory still makes me smile.

*   *   *

One day, my dad stopped by to bring me some money to buy disposable diapers, knowing that they would make it easier for me to care for Silva. After he got there, he realized that he didn't bring enough money. When he came back the next day with the rest, Kani and my mother-in-law got upset. "Why is he coming to visit you twice in one week?" they asked. I was hurt and confused why I couldn't even have my father over to visit twice in one week without their complaints.

While my dad was there, he noticed my breathing was heavy and labored. A couple of days later, he sent my mom to check on me. "Is everything okay?" she asked.

"Yes mom. Nothing to worry about. I am doing fine. Just feeling heavy from my pregnancy," I told her. Even though deep inside I desperately needed to talk to someone, I felt that doing so would only make things worse.

My parents didn't believe me though. Mom witnessed the way Kani treated me and my dad knew my breathing wasn't normal, even for a pregnant woman. They sensed something wasn't right, but they couldn't do anything. They had no hard evidence of a problem, and I wouldn't admit that anything was wrong. I just didn't want to create more tension in my troubled marriage.

*   *   *

Sevag was in Syria when the time came for me to have the new baby. My mom was in Saudi Arabia and my father was not home. When my water broke, I left Silva with my mother-in-law and rushed to the hospital by myself in a taxi. I felt sad and scared on the way there. I was all alone and just sixteen. My mother-in-law could have gone with me if we had left Silva with a neighbor.

Although the staff was shocked to see me enter the hospital without any family with me, I put my chin up, acting like I wasn't scared or sad about that as I entered the delivery room. After several hours of labor, following the birth I passed out, just like what happened when Silva was born.

When I woke up, I looked proudly upon my son, Hagob. He was in the nursery in an incubator, where they said he needed to stay for a day.

He was long and had lots of dark hair. I was ecstatic to have a son and thought that maybe Sevag's family would finally start to appreciate me.

The next day, I got up, put on my makeup, and did my hair. I was still feeling the euphoria of having a baby boy. I believed that things were going to change at home. A new, happier chapter of my life was about to begin. I felt like the world was mine.

The day after that, I saw my son's doctor pass my room as I sat on the bed. It was strange that he hadn't stopped in and that they hadn't brought Hagob to my room yet. I walked over to the nursery to check on my son. When I saw that there was another baby in my son's incubator, I immediately knew something was wrong.

Both my father and my husband, who had since returned from Syria, were there. Sevag tried to comfort me by telling me that the other baby was Hagob, but I knew that he wasn't. Right then, tears started streaming down my face. Finally, he admitted that baby Hagob had died. I never even had the chance to hold him.

All the hope my little angel had given me was stripped away in an instant. The doctors said that he was born with a hole in his heart. His death left me with a hole in mine. Losing baby Hagob was also hard on Sevag. I could see how upset he was.

I left the hospital quietly asking God for strength and I blamed myself for my son's death. I thought back to all the incapacitating abdominal cramps I had throughout my pregnancy. Sometimes I would climb six stories holding Silva, a baby bag, and stroller when the elevator to the apartment was broken. I felt I should have demanded to receive proper prenatal care.

During my hospital stay, the doctor asked Sevag and my dad if I was going through any kind of traumatic stress, which led Sevag to take me and Silva to his aunt's house in the mountains of Damascus in Syria. It was such a relief to be away from my mother-in-law and Kani for a couple of weeks and, as a result, I felt closer to him than ever before. It felt good knowing that he did something nice for me.

Those few weeks in the mountains were blissful in comparison to our everyday life back in Beirut. His aunt was very kind and allowed me to get some much needed rest and really catch my breath for the first time since my brother-in-law Hagob's death. During that visit, I also noticed that Silva's health was starting to improve. She was sleeping and eating better. Perhaps Silva was feeling better because I was feeling better.

The only way I knew how to deal with the loss of my son was to allow myself to grieve in a healthy way. I learned that grieving can take over our emotions to the point that we can't *see* what's happening around us. I've witnessed it turning into depression several times, which happened to my mom and mother-in-law. Both were victims of grief.

Focusing on my daughter was my main priority. As a mother, I needed to fulfill my role well and be present for her, instead of making her pay the price for my grief. Placing my attention on her helped me recognize how much she needed me, and that compelled me to take responsibility.

Sevag was also going through a lot. He was still grieving the loss of his sister and brother, along with losing his baby son, all of whom passed away in a short period of time. He too needed to get away from his family. Although I felt closer to him than ever before, we still didn't have a healthy husband-wife relationship. We couldn't discuss our feelings of grief at length, yet I embraced our peaceful time together.

I dreaded having to go back to Beirut. As soon as we did, things went right back to the way they were before I had the baby. Actually, they became worse. Without big Hagob around to defend me and baby Hagob, the son who I thought would bring me respect, Kani treated me like a piece of dirt.

As I was mourning the loss of my son, Kani and my mother-in-law were making nasty comments to other people and me. They couldn't understand why I was crying. "He was just a baby. It's not like you raised him," they would say. "You didn't even hold him." Still deeply sad from losing my baby son, they would stab a knife into my already broken heart with her hurtful comments. Being back at my in-laws' house made me feel like a prison inmate, ready to be discharged after serving a long sentence, but then was forced to serve an even longer term.

In light of the doctor's comments at the hospital, my dad made sure to check in on me regularly. I wanted so badly to open up to him, but I was afraid of the repercussions. Even though I wouldn't tell him what was going on, he sensed something was wrong . . .

CHAPTER ELEVEN

This Too Shall Pass

The pressures of home continued to build up. My husband was still not working except for an occasional day at the family store which Kani was managing. For the most part, he was relying on his family to take care of us.

After a long three and a half year struggle with my husband and his family, I just couldn't take it anymore. I went to my dad and opened up a little bit about what was going on. He suggested that we go to the priest who married us. Maybe he could help us find a solution to make our marriage work. My dad and I went to see the priest, who called Sevag and asked him to meet us for a family discussion. He soon showed up.

His family hadn't always been better off than us. Their first home, which they still had, was a small one located in an older area. I suggested to the priest and Sevag that we could live there. My older brother Elie could help us paint and fix it up. I thought it would be a nice home for us. I felt we needed our own space. Sevag agreed. *"Wow. I should've gone to the priest a long time ago,"* I told myself quietly.

I was so happy when we left the priest's home. I felt like I had finally gotten through to my husband. I thought we were going to move and I wouldn't have to deal with Kani and my mother-in-law any longer.

Not even an hour later, Sevag looked at me and said, "Don't think that what we talked about tonight is actually going to happen. I'm not going to leave a big, beautiful home for a tiny, rundown place. You can't take care of a house anyway. You can't even cook. I'd have to come to my mom's house every day to eat, so what would be the point? I'm not going anywhere."

"I'll learn how to cook. I'll do *anything* to make things better between us," I repeatedly pleaded. Suddenly, I realized the truth. It wasn't going to work. I didn't know what to say or do. I was out of ideas and options and felt completely alone.

My hopes were crushed. I couldn't understand why he agreed to move while in front of the priest and then did a complete one-eighty after we got home. I felt he was being totally unreasonable. I was so disappointed knowing that I'd have to live with my in-laws for a long time.

Sevag made me feel like I wasn't smart or good enough for him. In his eyes, I wasn't capable of doing anything. All I wanted to do was to keep my family together.

Confused and isolated, I started having anxiety attacks. Sometimes the attacks got so bad that the neighbors had to take me to the hospital. The doctors couldn't find any physical cause for my problems. Perhaps my issues were emotional, and the result of keeping everything bottled up inside. It's easier to prove physical abuse to someone than emotional abuse. No matter how hard I tried to tell my husband about what was happening, the response was always the same. He'd constantly tell me, "It's all in your head. You need to get over it."

As a result, I started having more breakdowns. I was spiraling downward, having flashbacks of all the loved ones I had lost. My anxiety attacks worsened. I would shake and hyperventilate. I was physically exhausted and so depressed. Above all, the enormous pressure of Kani's mental abuse started to push me over the edge.

Around that time, Sevag's uncle from the United States came to Lebanon. During his visit, everyone gossiped a lot. I wasn't sure what was going on, but whatever it was, the family did not want me to know about it.

It appeared that Sevag had become completely brainwashed by Kani. It seemed that he sincerely believed that I was some sinister temptress who used him to have a nicer place to live. He started acting like he felt that he had made a mistake and began to emotionally shut me out of his life completely.

The pressure and tension became horribly thick. I was being pushed so hard that it felt like I was suffocating. It seemed like they were working even harder to push me away. *Something is going on. I've got to go visit my dad and tell him everything.*

When I got to his place, I weeped as I finally let it all out. I told him how I had promised Silva that I would always keep her family intact. I didn't want to leave my husband, but if things continued the way they were going, my daughter wasn't going to have a mother. I needed help to make things better in my marriage, so I called Sevag from my dad's house to ask him to meet so we could talk.

"No, I'm not meeting you. You left, so you can just stay where you are. We have nothing to talk about!" he yelled, quickly hanging up the phone.

I wasn't planning on leaving him. All I had wanted to do was come over here and speak to my dad. Sevag knew that I only had the clothes on my back and the ones on Silva. It's not like I was planning to leave. I was searching for a solution for *our* marriage. It seemed that he was looking for an excuse to keep me away and was trying to convince himself that I had walked out on him. Dad advised me to call the priest again to let him know that I did not want to leave my husband. I was willing to do anything for a solution that would keep my family together.

*   *   *

Several days later, I was standing in the living room with my daughter wondering what I was going to do next. When my dad walked into the house, he had a deep look of concern on his face. He was silent for about three seconds and then said, "I have some news about your husband."

"What's going on?" I asked.

"Aimmee, this is going to be very difficult for you. At the same time, I know you're strong and can handle it," he said.

"What's wrong dad?" I asked with concern. "What's happened to my husband?"

"Well, Sevag has left Lebanon. He went to the United States."

My knees went limp and I fell to the chair beneath me. I held my daughter close. Every dream I had for her was crushed. I was absolutely stunned. *How could he leave and abandon his daughter? If he sincerely thought I was so terrible, then why did he leave his daughter with me? Why would he leave his own flesh and blood?* It was hard to accept that my daughter and I meant nothing to him.

Here I was living in the middle of the war as a single teenage mom with no education, skills or money. I didn't know what to do. I had no choice but to stay with my struggling family in their tiny one bedroom apartment. Still, I was grateful to have a place for us to stay. The most difficult thing was that I brought shame to my family and still had to deal with the culture's belief system, which looked down on divorced women.

A couple of days later, I went back to my mother-in-law's house to get my belongings. No one said anything to me as I walked in. I cried the whole time as I packed mine and Silva's clothes.

Now that Sevag was gone, I felt guilty for going to see my father that day. I thought that if I had been stronger and had kept everything to myself, I would still have a husband and my daughter's father would still be here. Perhaps I should have just dealt with everything on my own.

I realized that Sevag must have been planning his trip for a while. In those days, it would have been impossible to get a visa and ticket within the three days that I was at my dad's house before Sevag fled the country. He had done the same thing to me that he did to his family when he had gotten married. He wasn't man enough to tell me what he was planning, so he sneaked out and left Lebanon.

At that time in Lebanon, divorce was still a very uncommon thing. Divorcées stood out, especially when they were young and vibrant like I was. *Why would your husband leave you? You must have done something wrong.* That's what people were thinking when they looked at me.

Upon my return to my family's house, something remarkable happened. While Elie and I were sitting down in the living room and watching one of our favorite shows, for no apparent reason, he shut off the TV. I looked at him curiously. He took a deep breath, looked at me and said, "I apologize for everything that I did to you in the past. I promise I'll never lay a hand on you again." Naturally, I started tearing up. His eyes shifted down to the floor as he felt the guilt and shame of what he had done. It was incredible seeing the power of what he acknowledged and how he came out of his shell. Watching the burden lift off of his shoulders was euphoric, and I felt relief in both of our souls.

Witnessing his courage and seeing the freedom it gave us was life changing. His upfront and bold apology gave us a newfound freedom. He continued, "I'll also help you get back in school and raise your daughter." From that experience on, I deeply understood the *power* of an apology.

* * *

Elie kept his word in every way, and even paid for three months of French classes for me. After I had been attending a week, dad walked into the house. I could tell he wasn't feeling well by his yellow face. Then, I saw him quickly take his heart medication and noticed that his hands were trembling. That's when I got really concerned.

"I can tell something is wrong. What's the matter?" I asked.

"Elie fell at work and he's in critical condition," he said quietly. "He's at the hospital. Let's go." Dad refused to go into details about the accident.

Together, we quickly rushed to check on Elie.

When we arrived, his friends were standing in the lobby talking amongst themselves. Then, I heard one of them tell the other, "Elie has passed away." Upon hearing those words, I blacked out.

I was heartbroken and wished that Elie had never apologized. In some ways, I wished he had never offered to help. Maybe then I wouldn't have felt so devastated about losing him. My anxiety attacks quickly returned. Just months after my husband had left, I lost another brother. He was only twenty four. At the same time, I was happy knowing that he left this world with peace in his soul. This was very comforting.

You can only imagine how overwhelmed I was. I wanted to hang on to anything that would help me cope. Then, I realized who God had given me to get me through the darkness, my precious daughter. I had always protected her and now Silva was protecting *me*. My love for her kept me going. Having her with me was a gift from above. Whenever I went through a tough time, I always looked for my *why* . . . a reason that would help me move forward.

*   *   *

The last six months of Elie's life had given me hope. Our newly found brother-sister relationship had been deeply meaningful and healing. During that time, we had become best friends. Often when he got home from work, he had candy for Silva. He loved her so much. It seemed as though Elie was making up for his actions in the past by treating Silva extra special. He wanted to give us the best life possible.

Elie knew it wasn't my fault that Sevag left and that I hadn't done anything to bring shame to our family. He had told me, "I know that there are two sides of the story and your side is that you are a young, loving and forgiving person."

I often wondered what Elie was thinking as he fell six stories to the ground. The thought drove me crazy. Even now, when I see someone falling from a building on TV, I think of him. Like Robert, Elie also had a motorcycle, which remained parked in front of our apartment building after he died. Every time I hear the revving of a motorcycle, I think of Robert and Elie.

Elie never knew how he influenced my understanding of one's desires and wishes. One week before he died, Elie came home from attending a funeral. He started sharing his feelings about it with me and said,

"When I was there, I walked up and looked at the body. At that moment deep in my heart, I wished I could know what he was experiencing right now." Elie wanted to know what dying felt like. He wished to trade places with his dead friend so he could experience that moment.

"Brother, why are you telling me this?" I asked. "That's not something that you should wish for."

Despite my warning, his wish came true. About a week after his friend's funeral, Elie was gone.

Time and time again, I've seen that *making a wish from your heart can create reality.* The lesson of wishing was confirmed by my brothers Elie and Robert. They both had wished for the same thing; wanting to die. The old cliché is true; *be careful what you wish for.*

*   *   *

Mom's bitterness towards my father grew deeper. Shortly before Elie's death, dad had invented a mechanism to reduce industrial pollution by removing smoke and other pollutants from factory stack pipes. He found an investor to finance the project in a nearby factory where Elie got a job.

The day before Elie died, he came home from work, sat on the couch, propped up his feet, and told us that he had found himself an inch away from death earlier that afternoon. No one wanted to go up to the six story roof to clean the drain except for Elie. He never feared death, and heroically decided to make the ascent. He got the job done, but almost fell from the tile roof in the process. Elie got a big pat on the back for his bravery from the factory manager, a friend of dad's from France.

Unfortunately, when Elie made the climb again the next day, he wasn't so fortunate and fell six stories to the ground. Consequently, dad's friend felt guilty for allowing him to go up there a second time without a scaffold or ropes to secure him. One of dad's inventions had played an indirect role in the death of his son. Mom would never let him forget that.

*   *   *

Losing Elie was the most difficult for my mother. She was still living in Saudi Arabia with Jacque when the accident occurred. As you know, Elie and mom were close and had a lot in common.

My parents' apartment was too small for a proper viewing for Elie, so we had it in the lobby. He was dressed in a suit and placed on a bed. After the pallbearers made his casket dance in the air, like they did for Serune and Hagob who also died unmarried, young men fired their guns in the air. Similar to what they do during military funerals, the gunfire is a sign of respect and represents anger and sorrow.

My mother broke down at the gravesite. Losing Elie was too much for her. Mom had a hard time accepting that neither Robert nor Elie could come home to receive their proper final respects. She cried wishing that Elie had gotten married and left her with a grandchild. Elie was laid to rest next to Robert. As they lowered his body into the ground, I thought to myself, *"Elie, your brother and best friend is next to you. You are not alone."*

It seemed like every chance I had to stop wearing black, another event occurred, forcing me to wear it all over again. Dealing with one bad thing after another was difficult, but I didn't have time to sit and dwell on my sadness. I had to stay strong for Silva and my younger brother Roger.

In the early 1980s, mom returned to Beirut to attend Elie's funeral and pass the traditional mourning period of forty days. Following her visit, she and Roger returned to Saudi Arabia together.

My father was experiencing many trials. Along with being troubled by the war, he was grieving over his deceased loved ones, problems in his own marriage and my separation. Above all, dad was feeling guilty about not being in a better financial situation. That didn't stop him from opening his heart and home. He allowed Silva and me to stay with him even though he couldn't afford to feed us. He was struggling just to support himself, yet he made sure that I had some money in my pocket, and that Silva and I were taken care of. He became a father figure to Silva.

I felt bad about being separated from my husband and having to rely on my dad. Nevertheless, I swallowed my pride and went to Kani's store to ask her if she would help me take care of my daughter.

"What makes you think I would help you?" she asked.

"I am not asking you to help me. I am asking you to help your niece," I said. "My brother just died and my father is dealing with a health issue. He is helping me as much as he can. My husband left me with nothing and I have no way to feed my daughter."

"If you want help, you need to follow your husband to the United States and get him to help you. That's the only way you're going to get help," she said sarcastically.

She knew it would be almost impossible for me to go to the U.S. If I couldn't find money for food, how on earth could I make it there with Silva to get help from Sevag?

"This is Silva's uncle's store. Hagob would have wanted her to be raised properly. He would help her if he were still alive," I said.

"You'll have to get down on your knees and kiss my feet before I'll think about helping you!"

"You want me to beg you to help your own family? I will die before I do that."

Kani and I argued for a long time before I left the store. A week later, I swallowed my pride again and went to my mother-in-law's house to ask her to help me with Silva. She knew my family's situation and that we were in the midst of war. *"I'm sure she will understand,"* I told myself.

"I will only help her if she stays with me and you don't see her anymore," she said.

"No thank you," I replied. "My daughter is my life. I'll find a way to survive."

I had always treated her with respect. I couldn't understand why she was so cold and bitter towards me. The only possible reason I could think of was that Kani had successfully brainwashed her and turned her against me.

I carried my little girl on my shoulder and walked away. I wasn't sure how Silva and I were going to make it through. *What do I need to do? Where should I go? How can I make our lives work?*

As I was walking home, the bombs started up again. My inner and outer world were at odds and it felt like both were collapsing. A war wasn't only going on in my country, a different one was also taking place inside of me. I was scared, disappointed, and confused. All I wanted to do was to disappear.

The only thing I knew for sure was that I had to *conquer* my fears and find a way to survive somehow. I kept telling myself, *"This day shall pass."*

CHAPTER TWELVE

The Power Of My Why

My life was being taken over by fear. The memory of Robert's horrible death still haunted me. Every three to four weeks, I found myself dropping down on my knees, hunched over with my head to the floor. I sobbed uncontrollably and blamed everything that happened on the war.

There came a day when I had simply had enough. Blaming was only a temporary solution for coping with my emotional baggage. *I need to do something about my life. I can't continue this way.* I wanted to get help and decided that I was going to make it happen somehow. Immediately, I ruled out going to a therapist. Doing so was financially impossible. I needed more than that. *What can I do? Where I can go?* Finally, I got the answer.

I need to go to church. Why didn't I think of that before? I have to tell you, I was so excited! I couldn't wait until Sunday arrived. That morning, I woke up early and gave my daughter a bath. We both put on our nicest clothes. I felt optimistic and good about the idea of getting help.

The service had just started when we walked into the church. As I was walking toward my seat, I got goosebumps all over. I felt the love of God and an unbelievable sense of peace and calmness.

When the preaching began, the priest told us to turn to a certain page in the Bible. I quickly became uncomfortable and start panicking.

I couldn't find the page. A nice older woman was sitting next to me and noticed that I was struggling. She kindly reached over and helped me find the scripture. Finding the page was the easy part. Reading the Bible was another story.

When the time came to sing, I could not follow the words and keep up with everyone. I felt embarrassed and sick to my stomach, just how I felt at school. I wanted to go back into my shell and hide forever. When the service ended, I felt relieved.

I knew in my heart that feeling that way was not going to serve me or my daughter. I reminded myself of how much she needed me. Quietly I was thinking, *"I've got to find a way to conquer my fear."* I meditated and prayed about it. When I did that, I felt incredibly peaceful. The answer was right in front of me, something that I had practiced before. All I had to do was turn my fear *into* faith. My love for my daughter pushed me to find the solution. She was my life and my *why*!

*   *   *

One morning, I woke up to good news. My family had sent a visa and two plane tickets so Silva and I could visit them in Saudi Arabia. I didn't know what to do or think. I was so happy that I was going to see my family and get a break from the war. It was a joyful day that I would never forget. I felt that my prayers were answered.

Silva and I traveled between Saudi Arabia and Lebanon every time we got a chance. One day, the bombing got really heavy for a two or three day stretch. We prepared to flee for Saudi Arabia the next chance we could. The moment they announced a ceasefire on the radio, I quickly threw things in a suitcase, grabbed Silva and we took a taxi to the Beirut airport.

On the way, the ceasefire was broken and the bombing picked up again. Out of fear, I shouted, "It's not safe anymore! Take us back home!"

The taxi driver confidently replied, "No, we're so close. Don't worry. I'll get you to the airport safely."

We were the only car driving on the streets. He drove recklessly trying to avoid the bombs. More than anything, I was scared for my daughter's safety so I ducked down and covered her body to protect her from harm. It was the natural thing for a mother to do. Fear sank in and I had to remind myself of how important it was to turn my fear into *faith*. Finally, we made it to the airport safely. The bombing continued to get worse. We were fortunate enough to catch the very last flight. After that, the airport was shut down for several months.

* * *

We were grateful to be safe and sound with family in Saudi Arabia. However, there were adjustments to be made. Saudi Arabia is completely Muslim. My home country's population is a mixture of Christians and Muslims. In fact, Lebanon's president was required to be a Christian. Saudi Arabia's rules and customs were extremely different from those of Lebanon.

Saudi Arabia was a very beautiful place. The streets were clean and modern. Their malls and restaurants were very high end. The peace and security I felt there was wonderful.

Being a woman in Saudi Arabia had numerous limitations. First of all, there were significantly fewer job opportunities for women than in Lebanon. Unlike Muslim Saudis, Lebanese Muslim women do not cover their faces and whole bodies with black veils. At most, they wear a head covering, similar to what a Catholic nun wears. Women in Lebanon were allowed to drive and vote. Neither of those liberties was possible in Saudi Arabia.

Jacque was unable to do women's hair in Saudi Arabia as he had done in Lebanon. His specialization was in women's hair, not men's. The Saudi custom was that women could not let a man, other than their husbands, see them with their heads and faces uncovered. For this reason, Jacque could not do his line of work there. Mom did her best to help him in his struggling wholesale business.

Jacque was a smart, kind man. He had always been the artistic type and wasn't really cut out for business. As a result of his extended travel to Armenia as a kid, Jacque didn't read or write much Arabic. This made his job opportunities in Saudi Arabia limited and was a great source of stress. Futhermore, he was burdened by the significant debt he incurred to help support his family, which by then included a wife, son, and daughter.

Roger, who was still a kid, was also working in Saudi Arabia. Like me, he had to leave school. He got so far behind that continuing wasn't possible. The war had affected everyone and swiped away my little brother's educational opportunity. It broke my heart that Roger, the youngest of us all, had been unable to finish school. From the time he was ten, he had been helping sailors fix and clean their ships at Jeddah, a major Saudi port.

Dad traveled back and forth between Lebanon and Saudi Arabia. I could see how terrible he was feeling about the family's financial trouble. This only made his health decline even faster. He always wanted to provide us with a good life. His youngest son was working and unable to attend school. His wife was working at an age when she shouldn't have been. These circumstances made him feel like a failure.

Fortunately, mom was one of the few women who could find a job and was able to make some income. In addition to helping Jacque, she worked as an embroiderer in a ladies' clothing store, which was owned and operated by a woman. Jacqueline and my brother-in-law stepped in and helped our family in various ways.

Once while I was visiting mom at her job, her boss saw me and offered me some modeling work. She put me in a wedding dress and made me the main model in a private bridal fashion show. Some girls got jealous since they had been modeling for a long time and had more experience than me. I could hear the whispering that went on between them. *Why does she get to wear the wedding dress? She's never done this before. She doesn't know anything about modeling.* Even though I was grateful for the small amount of money the job generated, I was unhappy. I had no confidence in myself. I didn't fit in and felt like an outsider. I couldn't compete with the other girls. They were well dressed, educated and spoke to each other with confidence.

As soon as the event was over, I asked mom, "Can I go home? I don't want them to get to know me. I don't want them to know that I can't read or write, or that my husband ran out on me."

My heart was crying. *Here I am a young woman with no hope!* I didn't realize that I just pushed away an opportunity for me to make a decent living. Some of us are really good at recognizing that *opportunities* are around us all the time yet my fear kept opportunties *hidden* in a blindspot.

It was unusual to find a single woman from another country in Saudi Arabia. This made me stick out like a sore thumb at Lebanese community parties. I was always the only woman without a husband.

Even with all the problems I faced, I managed to make a good friend named Maya. Her husband was named Elie, like my brother. They were both very nice and kind. They also had a daughter the same age as Silva. Seeing her with a friend her own age she could play with made me feel good. Sometimes, we would stay at their house. For the most part though, I felt lost in that big country. Still in my early twenties, I hadn't found where I belonged in Lebanon. I couldn't find my place in Saudi Arabia either. Nevertheless, I was counting my blessings. I learned to focus on what I *have*, not on what I didn't have. Thinking that way helped me cope and go on with everyday life.

Even though I was counting my blessings, it didn't stop me from developing an attitude toward men. I was a fairly attractive young woman. However, as soon as they found out I was basically divorced (having been abandoned by my husband) and had a child, their view of me changed. They no longer considered me as someone they could take home and introduce to their family. Instead, they looked at me as a possible girlfriend to have fun with or a mistress. Unfortunately back then, that was the opinion of many Middle Eastern men. It got to the point that I hated being pretty and all the attention it brought. I just wanted happiness, peace, and a stable life. I didn't appreciate my young age or vibrance. I would have traded them in a heartbeat for a good education and a loving husband. Sadly, my attitude and personal beliefs about men were shutting down every opportunity I might have had.

* * *

While I was going back and forth between Saudi Arabia and Lebanon, I was looking for a potential father figure for my daughter. I wanted someone to save us both from our unstable lifestyle. Unfortunately during that time in the early 1980s, it wasn't acceptable to have a boyfriend, and you couldn't openly admit it if you did. You either had a husband or a fiancé. That's it. This made it exceptionally difficult to date. I had no freedom and felt like I was under constant scrutiny. I couldn't handle all the stares, whispers, and looks of disdain and judgment. I was confused and lost. I didn't know which direction to take.

Dealing with all the societal and financial pressures I was facing gave me a complex, which caused my blood pressure to plummet at times. Fortunately at the time, no one was collecting rent in Lebanon. The landlords understood that many people didn't have any money because of the war. Although I was able to live without paying rent, I still needed to feed and clothe my daughter.

* * *

When I got back to Lebanon, I was alone and desperately wanted my daughter to have family. I knew she needed love and attention. I chose to swallow my pride and go to my mother-in-law's apartment. During the first visit, Kani answered the door. Upon seeing me, she instantly put her hand on her hip and rudely asked, "What do you want?"

"I just want Silva to spend time with her family," I told her. She took her in and quickly shut the door.

For the sake of my child, I took her for another visit. Fortunately this time, Kani wasn't there and my mother-in-law invited me in for coffee. Little by little over time, our relationship started to change. I began to feel closer to her. She had been going through a lot. Within a short period of time, two of her children had died. She was also coping with her son's broken family and dealing with the war. If anyone could relate to her pain, it was me.

Deep inside I started to feel a lot of admiration for my mother-in-law. Despite my mistreatment in the past, I realized she was a strong woman who held her family together by dedicating her life to them. I started admiring her more and began looking up to her like a mother figure.

On another visit, Kani answered the door again but had less of an attitude. She greeted Silva, but still didn't invite me in. When I came to pick Silva up the next day, my mother-in-law asked, "Why didn't you come in for a visit yesterday Aimmee?"

Since I didn't want to say anything negative about Kani, I replied, "I had to do some errands."

She looked at me, smiled and said, "I miss it when you don't visit. Make sure you come in next time."

It felt good knowing that she looked forward to our visits. I left that day with a peaceful feeling. Our relationship had changed forever.

The following visit, Emhagob took me to the balcony and opened her blouse, which is what Middle Easterners traditionally do when saying sorry. She then proceeded to give me a heartfelt apology.

As she started to cry, she said, "My eyes were closed. I know I wasn't there for you and Silva. I refused to open my eyes and wake up. I did not make an effort to get to know you. I'm sorry about that. You're a good girl. Tell everyone I said so. I know you'll be there for me when I get older, but I wouldn't even expect Kani to bring me a cup of water."

I told her not to worry about the past and gave her a big hug. In the back of my mind, I knew that someday Kani was going to have a change of heart.

Whenever I would visit after that, my mother-in-law would cry when we talked about old times. I had always treated her well and she fondly remembered the time I lived with her as her best days. I had always been a lot nicer to her than Kani and I made her life easier by taking care of everything in the house when I lived there.

I really enjoyed it when Mary would be there too. I had always loved her. Being around her and Emhagob made me feel like I had a family again.

Despite my closeness to Mary and her, I never received any financial help from their family because Kani controlled the finances. They knew we were struggling, but I held my tongue. I didn't want to risk my newly created relationship with Emhagob.

On Sundays, the family often went to a restaurant. I liked Silva to go with them so that she could enjoy a good meal and a nice family social outing. I wasn't able to provide her with such luxuries.

One weekend, my mother-in-law gave me a jar of her homemade *tourshi batlijan,* pickled eggplants with nuts in oil. She had always been a great cook and often did lots of canning. She knew those pickles were one of my favorite snacks.

I was so glad to have something to eat since I didn't have anything in the refrigerator. I was so hungry when I got home, I borrowed some bread from my neighbor to go with the pickles and ate them all as quickly as I could. I ended up throwing everything up though. I hadn't eaten for several days, so my body rejected all the oil.

Over time, my relationship continued to deepen with my mother-in-law. Apparently her change of heart rubbed off on Kani. We started to get along better at least on the surface, to the point that I felt comfortable enough to occasionally stay at my in-laws' for the weekend. Kani's husband John was such a nice guy. He treated me very well and would treat Silva like he did his own two daughters, Silva's first cousins.

One Christmas, however, Silva spent the holidays with her grandmother and Kani's family. She noticed that her cousins got a lot more presents than she did. It hurt me that Silva was starting to realize that she was being treated differently than the other grandkids. I tried to reassure her that the whole thing was just an oversight and that no one meant for her to receive fewer gifts.

After a while, it became a struggle to take Silva over to her grandma's because she sensed she wasn't being treated fairly. But on the other hand, even though she received less than her cousins, she received much more at her grandmother's house than I could offer.

Meanwhile the whole family was prospering from Silva's deceased uncle's business, especially Kani who wore expensive designer clothing, shoes, and purses. She would also give lots of money to the Red Cross to look like a good Samaritan. Yet she never offered to help provide for Silva, except for getting her clothes on holidays and on her birthday.

Around that time, Silva had to be hospitalized for pneumonia and tuberculosis exposure. I didn't have any money, so I pawned the little bit of jewelry I had accumulated over the years to pay for her hospital bill.

The time she spent in the hospital occurred during a particularly heavy period of bombing. I was so worried sick about my daughter that the bombs didn't even phase me. When I'd leave the hospital, I'd walk through the streets unmoved and unaffected by the bombs flying overhead. I couldn't get in touch with any of my family in Saudi Arabia. This only intensified how lost I already felt.

A little while later, when the phone lines became available, I called my sister and asked her for help. Within a few days, I received money from her. I was thankful for her help, which gave me enough money to pay for the medication that Silva would need for a long period of time.

Along with the rest of Sevag's family, Kani visited Silva in the hospital and left the equivalent of twenty five dollars under her pillow to help with the bill. I was grateful for any help I could get, yet the amount Kani contributed paled in comparison to the size of Silva's hospital bill.

When my brother Roger found out the news about Silva, he came from Saudi Arabia to see her as soon as he could. He had always adored her so much. Just nine years apart, the two were close enough in age that they could have been brother and sister. Although he was still a kid too, he had been working in Saudi Arabia and used some of his money to buy presents for Silva. Roger treated her like his little sister, just like Robert treated me.

Meanwhile, Sevag's family told him that Silva was in the hospital. I had quickly gone home to shower and change clothes when he called.

Regardless of not receiving any support from him, it made me happy that he contacted her to show he cared.

Rumors were circulating that Sevag was dating many different women in the U.S. AIDS was a newly discovered disease back then and significantly on the rise, so his family, including Kani, wanted us reunited. They disagreed with his lifestyle and felt that he'd be better off putting his family back together.

Our divorce was not yet final. It takes a very long time to get one in Lebanon, especially when children are involved, due to all the church and legal proceedings required. It takes an even longer time when one party is nowhere to be found to sign the documents or to appear for questioning.

My father acted as my attorney during the proceedings. There were five or six higher-ups in the Armenian church in the room with my father and me. I felt like I was being interrogated as they asked, *"Why do you think he left? Do you want a divorce?"*

By that point I did want a divorce, but my in-laws convinced me to give it another try. Part of me still held on to the dream of having an intact family for my daughter, who was around five years old at the time. So, the day before the divorce was to be granted, I went to the church and asked them to put the case on hold . . .

CHAPTER THIRTEEN

Doing My Best

A common saying of ours was "If the first bomb doesn't hit you, you'll probably escape the second." It was usually true since we had learned how to seek shelter and secure ourselves within a split second of becoming aware of any trouble.

When the bombing picked up, we would immediately wake up in the middle of the night. While we were still half asleep, we'd drag ourselves along with our children and the elderly to safer territory. The kids would be crying and disoriented as they heard the buildings shaking and glass shattering. All of the neighbors would gather in the basement or on the steps in the middle of the building. You could see the exhaustion on everyone's faces. As soon as the sound of the bombs slowed down, we would lay down on the floor for a little while to take a nap.

Silva's safety was my number one priority. You can imagine how stressful it was raising a young daughter in a war-ridden country. Trying to get back with Sevag was an opportunity to get her away from the war and into a safe environment.

Despite my wishful thinking and hopeful thoughts, Sevag didn't seem very interested in bringing me to the U.S. Although he never said that he didn't want us to come, I felt no warmth from him during our conversations before Silva and I left Lebanon.

His family tried to reassure me that he was acting indifferent because he had been living a different lifestyle for so long. They felt the only way for him to get back to his traditional Armenian roots was for him to have his family with him.

"Aimmee, don't be scared", his cousin told me. "Your mother-in-law is going to fly to California a month before you. She will be there to help you with anything you need. She's going to prepare for your arrival and try to reign in Sevag's lifestyle."

My mother-in-law had always been a strong woman, a matriarch accustomed to having a significant say in her children's lives. Until he married me behind her back, she had always been successful with her influence.

His family had been trying hard to bring us back together. Perhaps they felt he was lost and alone in a foreign country. Looking back, I think he only agreed to let us come in order to please his family. It was the exact same thing that he used to do years earlier when he would ignore me.

We had secured five year tourist visas, yet my father insisted that I get roundtrip tickets. In case things didn't work out, he didn't want us to be stranded on the other side of the world. Sevag's cousins paid the fare and understood why I needed to secure the return tickets. I didn't expect to need roundtrip tickets though, as I was determined to put my family back together.

It had been several years since Sevag left Lebanon when Silva and I boarded the plane headed for Los Angeles, California. He was still my legally wedded husband. Throughout the sixteen hour flight, I kept trying to imagine how our reunion would be. I didn't know what to expect, but I hoped for the best. With all my effort, I earnestly tried to erase the sting of his abandonment. If we were going to work things out, I had to forgive him for the hurt and pain of the past.

The question was; *How do I do that?* I realized that the first step was to make a *choice*. In order to forgive him, either I was going to *focus* on the pain, or focus on the few good memories. I started thinking about the few good times I had with him, and how he used to come to see me every day at the church in Syria. He would ask me to go out with him and tell me how much he loved me.

I remembered when Sevag gave me a big hug and cried on my shoulder when he learned about his brother Hagob's death. He hung on to me and said, "I'm glad to have you in my life. I don't know what I would do without you."

I continued recalling more good memories, like when he took me to his aunt's house in the mountains after our infant son died. That way, I could recuperate and get a much needed break from his family, who at that time had all but completely rejected me. Choosing to focus on the positive memories helped me and gave me a sense of peace!

I felt like I was leaving behind the pain. I was hoping for a fresh new start with a bright future. As I sat in my seat and looked out the window, I marveled at how radically life can change. Unbelievably, his family, who was once in great part responsible for our breakup, was now entirely supportive of our getting back together. With his family's support, I felt strong and on top of the world. I always wanted their approval and I finally had it. What else could I have asked for? Life was good.

Sevag, his mother, and Susie, his half-American cousin, greeted us at the airport. He brought me flowers, yet I still sensed no affection from him. Since we hadn't seen each other in years, we were both nervous and uncomfortable. His mother however, greeted me with great affection, giving me a warm embrace and a kiss on both cheeks.

Sevag was surprised by his mother's dramatic change of heart. He felt compelled to say something about it. The last time he had seen us together, his mother only spoke to me when she wanted to put me down.

"What did you do to my mom to make her love you so much?" he asked me.

"All I did was continually give her love and compassion," I replied.

A week into my visit, Sevag had still hardly spoken two words to me. I tried to strike up conversations, but he would give me one-word, yes-no answers and wouldn't even take his eyes off the TV.

He still seemed to harbor resentment toward me. With Kani's help years ago, he had convinced himself that I had tricked him into the marriage.

I could see that he enjoyed having his daughter. I knew deep inside he wanted to have his family. However, the price was too high for him to pay.

If he was going to have us both, he would need to commit to the marriage. That would mean losing the lifestyle which he took so much pleasure in.

He was having fun dating women and didn't have a care in the world. Marriage would take all that away. Sevag didn't know which direction to take. Therefore, he put a wall around his heart and shut down his emotions. It was difficult to watch. Having a family comes with certain sacrifices, but unfortunately he wasn't willing to make them.

Meanwhile, I felt frustrated as Sevag ignored me even more than he did years ago. He still seemed to think that he was better than me. Even his mother got upset with him for his lack of attention and effort in trying to get reacquainted with his family. It quickly became painfully obvious that putting my marriage back together would be an exercise in futility. My hopes were crushed. I felt as rejected and unwanted as I did when he left us years ago.

Silva's deepening relationship with Susie worsened my feelings. With extra effort, she was trying her very best to get close to Silva and win her over. Even though I appreciated the attention she gave my daughter, something just didn't feel right.

A couple of times I received a phone call from an anonymous woman. She told me that Sevag and Susie were planning to do paperwork for Silva so she could stay in the U.S. They were also planning to send me back home to Lebanon. This confirmed the uneasiness that I had been feeling.

There was an even greater reason I was feeling threatened. In support of my suspicions, Sevag and Susie, who both spoke Armenian, would only speak English in my presence, so that I couldn't understand them. Sometimes though, I would have a fairly good idea about what they were saying based on their body language and eye contact. He thought he was pulling the wool over my eyes every time they spoke.

During a road trip we took to Las Vegas, he had Susie sit in the front seat, while I sat in the back with Silva and Emhagob. He said you had to have a driver's license to sit in the front seat on long trips, which even I knew was a ridiculous explanation. I felt highly disrespected being made to sit in the back, since I was his wife.

During the long drive, I sat looking out the window at the great desert expanse between Los Angeles and Las Vegas. The great natural beauty of the big, blue sky and the majestic mountains were lost on me as I cried inside. I could tell Emhagob wasn't happy either. Neither of us wanted to make a scene, especially with Silva there, so we both kept quiet.

Despite my feelings, I still wanted to try to work things out with Sevag. I wanted to put one hundred percent effort into rebuilding my family. I didn't want to feel guilty that I hadn't done everything possible to save it. I thought to myself that maybe he'd get over his close attachment to Susie. I didn't know how it would happen, but I wished it would for my daughter's sake.

After we arrived in Las Vegas, we checked in to our hotel and then freshened up to stroll The Strip. I got dressed up and looked good on the outside. However on the inside, I felt dark, sad, and depressed. The glitz and glamour of Las Vegas at night, aglow with millions of neon lights, did nothing for me. As we walked, I wondered why I was there and what I was doing.

Later that evening, we saw a glamorous, Parisian-style show. No matter how hard I tried to enjoy the moment, I simply couldn't do it. I was heartbroken and disappointed that my family wasn't coming together.

As it grew late, we returned to our hotel room. Emhagob quickly drifted off to sleep. I was so tired, but I sensed that Sevag and Susie were waiting for me to go to sleep, so that they could go out on the town without me. Sevag had already disrespected me during the long drive to Vegas and I didn't want to let him get away with that again. I tried with all my might to stay awake, knowing that he wouldn't have the audacity to leave while I was still up. But my body's need for rest won out. When I woke up several hours later, Sevag and Susie were gone.

Here I was in Las Vegas where people enjoy some of the most incredible scenery and lights in the whole world, yet I was laying in the hotel room feeling the darkness in my heart. I kept trying to figure out how to escape that darkness. Then I turned to my daughter, looked at her and saw the *light* through her eyes.

* * *

Back in Los Angeles, Susie would sometimes sleep at Sevag's one bedroom apartment with all of us; Sevag, Silva, me and his mother (even though she had her own place just a block away). It didn't make sense for her to sleep on the floor at Sevag's place since she had a comfortable bed at home. This kept confirming my concern of what people were telling me in private.

Susie and Sevag would stay up late chatting and enjoying their conversation, acting as if I were invisible. It didn't take too long for Emhagob to become so disillusioned with Sevag's new lifestyle that she all but gave up hope of seeing her son's family reunited. In a last-ditch effort, she thought that maybe if she left we'd have more privacy and could work things out. About three weeks into my visit, Emhagob departed disappointed and sad, clinging to one last hope. My heart went with her. I too was disappointed in how things had transpired up till then. Meanwhile, I continued receiving cautionary phone calls. Neighbors and friends were warning me to be careful and to hold on to Silva.

My daughter was my life and my why. She was the reason I was living and breathing. We were so close to each other, that separating us would have been devastating and heartwrenching for both of us. I knew I needed to *step up* and make a *choice* that would keep us together. I took a deep breath and then meditated and prayed. Deep inside, I knew the answer but still I had doubts. I told myself, *"Don't give up Aimmee. Talk to him."* I was desperately trying to give him the benefit of the doubt.

When I tried to talk to Sevag about my concerns, he would shut me down and wouldn't let the conversation go anywhere. I was already frightened by the rumors. His unwillingness to talk about plans for Silva scared me even more. Deep in my bones, I started to believe that there must have been some truth to the hearsay. At the same time, I couldn't understand why Sevag would suddenly want Silva to stay with him in the first place. He had never taken much interest in her in all the years before that. *"What's happening now?"*, I wondered.

Furthermore, his current lifestyle wasn't conducive to raising a child, particularly a young girl. It actually seemed like Susie was more interested in Silva, perhaps in an attempt to win Sevag's heart. I felt that if he genuinely wanted to have her in his life, he would have wanted to work out some sort of arrangement. It would be in Silva's best interest for us to work together, instead of him trying to take my daughter away from me behind my back.

Although we'd be returning to a war-torn country if we went back to Lebanon, we always held on to the hope that a ceasefire was on the horizon. We believed that peaceful times were coming soon. Therefore, I felt strongly that my daughter and I would be better off together no matter where we were. I still wanted Silva to have her father in her life. I had gone through so much trying to keep our family together. If Sevag had wanted to join forces to raise her without the ties of a relationship between us, I would have eagerly agreed to those conditions for her benefit. Otherwise, staying in the United States wasn't a realistic option for me.

In need of some advice, I called Sevag's cousins, the ones who had bought my plane ticket.

"I feel like I'm choking and all alone in a strange country. I'm constantly ignored and he refuses to communicate," I told them.

"Do whatever you think will be best for you and Silva," they said. "We understand if you have to return home."

They knew I had tried to do everything I could to work things out. They caught wind of how things were going from Emhagob, who by that time was back in Beirut.

Fear of losing my daughter had overtaken me. I wondered, *"If I'm not healthy, how can I be the best mom I can be?"* At the same time, it made me stronger. Sevag wasn't willing to sacrifice or compromise for his daughter, but I was. I carefully started to think about my choices.

As her mother, I had to protect her. I asked some local relatives to help me leave the U.S. without Sevag's knowledge. I was afraid that if he found out that we were leaving, he and Susie wouldn't allow me to take my daughter. It was my duty to do whatever I felt was in her best interest. My hopes and dreams were shattered, but my choices were not!

As I looked into Silva's eyes on our way to the airport, I was filled with mixed emotions. I felt sad that I wasn't able to work things out with her dad. On the other hand, I was glad that she had the chance to meet him and see a new country.

Stepping on the plane, I chose to leave with no judgement. I decided to give him the benefit of the doubt and assured myself, *"I have no idea what he is going through emotionally. I know I did my best. I tried everything I could. I have to stay healthy and keep peace in my heart and mind. Judging him will only hurt me. I don't know what's going on inside of him. Maybe he tried his best."* Choosing to think this way helped me to move on.

During the flight back home, I realized we were all alone. I would have to face the stigma of being a single young woman abandoned by her husband.

After the plane touched down on Lebanese soil, my daughter and I headed for our family's apartment. Tiny as the apartment was, it felt like a mansion as I thought back to the feelings of rejection and disrespect I felt during our visit with her father. I had no idea what I was going to do, but at the very least I was relieved and happy that my daughter and I were still together.

Those choices were very hard. Little did I know that more difficult decisions were lying ahead . . .

Chapter Fourteen

Escaping Death Again and Again

Dwelling on the disappointment over my U.S. visit was something I didn't have time for. Since I had a young daughter to take care of, I started looking for employment right away. However, before I could make that happen, I had to find someone to watch my daughter while I worked. Unable to think of anyone, I had to ask my mother-in-law for help.

"Can you help me with Silva if I find a job?" I asked, as I stood at her door.

"I would do that for you, but I honestly can't." she said. "I am already stressed out from watching my two other grandkids. My nerves can't handle another one. I'm getting too old to do all this."

I shook my head and replied, "I understand." I gave her a hug and walked away, feeling compassion for her. *I deeply believe that loving and forgiving are necessary for living a peaceful and happy life.*

Even though she was unable to watch my daughter, I still continued to visit them a couple times each month. After all, Emhagob had become like a mom to me. I had known her since I was fourteen. I also knew that my daughter needed to feel that she had a family who loved and cared about her. I knew how important it would be for her to feel the warmth, love and affection that only comes from family.

Before long, I got an opportunity to do stage acting in plays along with some modeling. I hoped that the modeling in Lebanon would be a better experience than doing so in Saudi Arabia.

Fortunately while I worked, I was able to leave my daughter with my parents who were in town from Saudi Arabia at the time. When she was out of school on the weekends, I would take her to the family-oriented plays. She enjoyed sitting in the audience watching me on stage.

I was grateful for the very small amount of income those jobs brought in. Like any career, when you work in modeling and acting, you have to build up your name before you can make a decent living. However, getting popular requires great self-confidence and I didn't have that. Many opportunities kept slipping away right in front of my eyes. I was so unsure of myself that I never really enjoyed the work and subconsciously I rejected it.

Feeling comfortable with all the socializing involved was almost impossible, especially the high society parties when people would talk about brand name clothing, purses, and makeup that I had never heard about.

Joining them in a fancy restaurant was even worse. You can only imagine how hard it was for me when the time came to order from the menu. In order to hide my reading difficulties, I became a master at making excuses. Before ordering my meal, I always used to lean towards the person sitting next to me and say, "Oh, I forgot my glasses. I can't see very well. What are you going to order?" Then, I would order whatever he or she was having.

I wasn't always able to hide. Although I was willing to make excuses and figure out ways around things, I refused to lie. When someone asked me which school I graduated from, I had to admit that I had minimal education. I also couldn't hide when I was auditioning for acting jobs. The moment I felt that they were going to ask me to read a script, I panicked and quickly found a way out to go hide in my shell.

This further diminished my self-confidence. In the back of my mind, I just kept hearing negative voices. *"You're not good enough to do anything.*

Who do you think you are?" I truly started to believe that I was nobody and lost my identity.

* * *

My parents were getting older and grew more heartbroken, lost and confused. The war had taken away every inch of happiness they had. They tried to do their very best though. They went back and forth to Saudi Arabia, trying to find a way to make a living.

Once again, I was alone in Lebanon staring at the walls wondering how I was going to make it. I was in my early twenties and the war was still going on.

Jobs were very limited. Fortunately, I found one even though many people with more skills and education were out of work. I was hired to do sales in a men's clothing store. I was so excited! Having a job filled me with hope.

All I needed to do next was to find someone who would watch my daughter when I went to work. Unfortunately, I was out of luck and couldn't find anyone to love and take care of her. I was forced to make the heart-wrenching decision to put her in boarding school. It was one of the most difficult decisions I ever had to make. Remembering my own boarding school experiences, I made sure to enroll her in a much better school than mine. I knew she'd be well taken of there, yet it still crushed me and completely broke my heart. I remembered how abandoned I felt while I was in boarding school away from my family. The thought of my daughter feeling the same way like I had really hurt. Leaving Silva alone at home during the war while I went to work was not an option. She was way too young to even walk back and forth to school or take care of herself. I needed to know she was safe with a trusted adult and I could only provide that by enrolling her in the boarding school.

I was excited and happy about my new job. *"Everything is going to be great,"* I told myself. *"I'll be making money and soon I'll be able to get Silva out of boarding school and hire a babysitter to watch her at home. I just need a couple of months to reach my goal."* I thought for sure that my job wouldn't require me to read or write. I was simply going to be selling suits, shirts and ties.

Surprise overcame me when the truth hit. I needed more education about the products, where they came from and their details. All of that required reading skills. The clothing tags were a mystery to me since they were written in English or French. I wanted to disappear especially when the time came to write out invoices for the customers. It became obvious that for me to be successful in that job, I'd have to know how to read and write. I couldn't escape that reality.

The boss kept me around for his own reasons. "There's a price for everything," he said, as he made his first pass at me. I politely and repeatedly declined his advances. A few weeks later, I decided to quit.

Following that experience, I felt alone and lost. I needed guidance and direction. I remember walking through the streets being completely out of it, lost in a haze. The only thing that got me back home safely was my prayers to God.

After a long job search, I found a position I thought I could handle as a hostess at a toy wholesaler. Most of my coworkers were educated and had been working there several years, yet they were still working behind the scenes. I was new and already working upfront, so it was understandable that some of them seemed to dislike and resent me. Before my arrival, they had worked up front from time to time. Following my hire, they were no longer allowed to interact with customers. That was my job. Being a hostess was a prized position. It required interaction with prominent business people and also paid more. Apparently, the boss wanted me to be the face of his business.

Little by little, the boss threw more responsibilities my way. An order here, a message there, something new to do . . . and each new task would require me to write. I quickly started feeling overwhelmed again. In an effort to hide my inability to read and write, I'd sneak in the back to open boxes and make one of my coworkers cover for me in front.

When my boss would find me, he'd ask, "Why are you back here?" I would explain that I didn't feel ready to be up front yet and suggest someone who would be a better choice.

"You're underestimating who you are," he'd reply. It was simple to understand why he said this. He viewed me as confident and capable. I walked and talked like an educated woman, but the truth was that he didn't accept my weaknesses, that I couldn't read and write.

Even though I was hiding in my shell when I did small tasks like writing a note, I still felt light glowing in my heart. People were attracted to the peace I had. They wanted to have that experience too while they were going through life's challenges and obstacles. Every time I reached out to help them have peace and joy, I saw the pressure lift off of their shoulders. It felt great doing this and I knew it was my gift. Unfortunately, I didn't have the educational opportunity to pursue my gift as a career so I was not able to help more people.

My appearance caused people to view me as being more educated than I really was. Like my boss, they didn't want to hear or accept the truth about my learning disabilities, which made me feel even more pressured to hide them. Instead of believing what they saw in me, I wanted them to belief my unhealthy thoughts about myself. I was trying to change *their* beliefs instead of *mine*.

When the toy store job inevitably did not work out, I tried to find a suitable job but couldn't. No one wanted to hire me for a behind-the-scenes job.

"You have a God-given beauty. You're smart and intelligent. You can't be stuck in the back. You deserve to be upfront in a good paying job," they would say. I felt like I was in limbo, stuck between the world's perception of me and my stark reality.

The negative voices would come to haunt me again. I felt like a prisoner held in my shell, a prison I had created. From it I could see the blue sky from the window, but couldn't go out and join the beauty of life.

It is amazing how unhealthy thoughts can take over and leave you stuck in your shell, waiting for something or someone to get you out. I chose to stay stuck in my prison for years, while helping others get out of theirs. If I had just paid attention and listened to my own advice, I would have been out enjoying the blue sky and what life had to offer. Back then, I didn't realize that I was holding *my own key* to freedom.

* * *

It was 1985 when I received a phone call from my sister Jacqueline.

"I have a job offer for you Aimmee!" she happily said. "My husband and I need to travel back and forth between the U.S. and Saudi Arabia for business. We need someone we can trust to watch the kids when we're gone. What do you think of that?"

"I would love to do it!" I happily replied. Right then and there, I agreed to give it a try. I was so excited! I felt this was a great opportunity for my daughter and me. We quickly received the plane tickets. I packed our belongings and we headed toward the airport. Leaving for the U.S. this time filled me with optimism and *hope*.

A couple of days after my arrival, I quickly discovered that I was in over my head. My sister lived in a rural area without any public transportation and there was no Middle Eastern community to help me get acquainted with the area.

Her life was very busy then, so she didn't have time to teach me how to do the things she needed me to do. As you know, I didn't speak English and I barely could read or write in Arabic. I couldn't take messages or do anything that would serve her such as taking care of her bills or driving the kids to school. It didn't take even a month for us to realize that the arrangement wasn't working out.

I was always uncomfortable sharing my problems and weaknesses with my sister, since I was compared to her all my life. Therefore, she didn't really know what I would be facing back home. I just didn't want Jacqueline to see me as a failure. The reality was that I needed a lot of training and experience before I could take over and help her with the kids. I felt disappointmented and overwhelmed, which allowed those unhealthy voices to come back and haunt me.

Although I had hoped that working for my sister would give me a fresh start in a new country to provide a better life for my daughter, we were soon boarding a plane headed back to Lebanon.

Not even a week later, I was in the kitchen with my mom and grandma. They were cooking kibbee, a traditional Middle Eastern dish. Kibbee was my favorite dish and they were making it to welcome me back home. I was enjoying the scent of the onions and spices and was happy to see my mom and grandma together, chatting and having a good time. Silva was happy to be playing with her best friend, Agaveny.

I was sitting by the kitchen window serving mom and grandma Turkish coffee. As I finished filling their cups, I felt the air lift me out of my chair, followed with a LOUD explosion. A huge car bomb had exploded behind our apartment building. In an instant, the windows shattered into bits and pieces as smoke filled the tiny apartment. Then there were seconds of pin-dropping silence that felt like an eternity.

During that lapse in time, my heart stopped beating as I looked back and forth between mom and grandma, wondering where my daughter and her friend were. I was panic-stricken, thinking that they had been on the balcony. My heart started beating again a second later when they came out from the bedroom where they had been playing. I was amazed that all of us were still breathing.

After that, all hell broke loose. You could hear screaming and crying everywhere. Cars screeched as people rushed to take their loved ones to the hospital. Mom started to lose it and hyperventilate, while grandma stood frozen in shock. Within seconds our survival instinct kicked in. As we headed for the door, we saw that it had caved in from the pressure. We had to squeeze through a small opening to get to safety in the basement, three stories below.

As we rushed to get underground, we met up with Agaveny's mother on the street. People were panicking and running around screaming, covered in blood as they carried loved ones off to safety or the hospital. Body parts were scattered here and there, from people who were strolling the streets just moments before.

In an attempt to hide the gore from my daughter, I held her close, keeping her face toward my body. But there was too much bloodshed, making it impossible to keep her from seeing what was going on. I was so scared. The memories of the bomb that killed Robert started flashing before my eyes as I realized that I had escaped death again.

That car bomb was so powerful that it destroyed three big buildings and even made the news in the U.S. Despite my efforts to hide it from her, Silva distinctly remembers that car bomb to this day.

*　　*　　*

The bombings were completely unpredictable. When they started up again, we'd all kick into survival mode. We would flee, doing whatever it took to get everyone to safety. You'd see mothers everywhere running to school to grab their kids, and then hurrying home with their children crying and shivering from fear. Once there, they anxiously waited and prayed to God for their husbands and fathers to return safely.

The land lines would go down, cutting us off from all communication with loved ones. Keep in mind that we're talking about the early 1980s when cell phones weren't available.

Lebanese people are very resilient. Surprisingly, we adapted the best we could to living surrounded by war. We still had weddings and parties to *keep our spirits up*. We took trips to the beach and the mountains, and sometimes went out dancing. Whenever we heard a bomb strike, we'd hide in a beach cabana if we were at the ocean or pull to the side of the road if we were driving. We'd tune in to the radio for information and stay put until the news said the threat had died down. Ultimately, we'd continue doing whatever it was we were doing, in business-as-usual style.

We had to keep moving forward and living. The war taught us how to live *every moment* as if it were our last. Collectively, we knew how precious life was because each of us had lost someone we cared about. Perhaps we savored life to the fullest as we knew firsthand how abruptly it could end.

At the same time, we did live in fear. Walking in Beirut was like walking through a minefield. Every building was scarred from the bombings and had walls of sandbags in front of the entrance to protect people entering. The roads were not being maintained and their many holes would fill with water when it rained. Water would splash everywhere when cars would drive over the potholes.

Car bombs were everywhere and often destroyed two or more buildings. We'd rush by every car, hoping and praying each time that the one we passed wasn't rigged with an explosive device. The traffic lights weren't working either, leaving the streets in chaos. Besides the ever-present war, my daughter was going through her own problems around that time. She felt like an outsider because she didn't have a father around like all of her friends. Holidays and special occasions were especially difficult for her and I could see the sadness in her eyes. She was getting older and consequently starting to understand and feel the pain of the war.

Fortunately, my grandma, Silva's great grandma, was a comfort for her around that time. When we used to visit her, she would fix us a hot meal, which was a much-welcomed simple pleasure. I remember how Silva would often hold her great grandma's hand as they crossed the street together. When grandma wasn't feeling well, Silva would comfort her and bring her something to drink. I was proud of the way Silva treated her great grandma and other elderly people, which made me love her even more.

I loved my daughter so much and wanted to be the best mom I could be. Of course mothers love their children, but it was obvious that my love for her was over the top. She was everything to me and had a special way of making me feel good. On top of that, she was also very cute and lovable. I intentionally didn't have many friends so that I could spend as much time with her as possible. People would cast a strange look at me when they saw how doting and overprotective of her I was. They said that I was like a mother cat holding her kitten by the nape of the neck.

* * *

During a two week period of no bombing, everyone started to let their guard down as usual. We thought the war was about to end. We even started to allow our kids to play in the nearby playground.

One day, my daughter was playing with her friends, when suddenly, the bombs started picking up again. When I heard the first one, I immediately went into a panic, worried about her well-being. Within minutes I found myself running down the stairs, struggling with the other mothers to get to our kids. We almost trampled each other as we ran to the playground. I wished I could fly to get to my daughter and was overcome with fatigue after I discovered she was all right. The emotional trauma I experienced for the couple of minutes it took to get to her was so tiring. Although the playground was only a building away, it felt like I had just run a marathon.

* * *

It was New Year's Eve. Mom and dad were both home in Beirut. Silva was visiting with Grandma Emhagob while my mother and I headed to a New Year's Eve party with some friends. Mom went in one car and I rode in another that followed. As we drove along the freeway, we were confident that we'd be safe. My friends and I were chatting and looking out the windows, eager for the driver to point out the area where a car bomb had exploded earlier that day.

As we got closer, my friend got a little impatient. Mom's car in front of us was going fairly slow, so my friend decided to pass them. Just before we passed their car, BOOM! Another car bomb exploded in the exact same spot as the one earlier that day. It instantaneously erupted into a huge fire. Within seconds, the car in front of my mom's was completely destroyed. At the same time, a big piece of wood dropped on our car, shattering the windshield. The broken glass went everywhere.

Traffic came to a standstill and a frenzy broke out. It was total chaos with cars crashing left and right, horns honking, and people getting out of their cars looking around in bewilderment. Everyone was in a panic. No one could believe that a car bomb had exploded in the same spot twice in same day. That had never happened before.

As I looked ahead to my mom's car, another vehicle had hit hers on the side, drastically caving in the door. Her car looked almost completely destroyed. I saw my mom panicking, trying to get out by banging against the inside of the car door. Trapped inside, she was completely freaking out, pulling her hair and screaming, "Get me out!" I feared that her legs had been broken or severed. My body started shaking uncontrollably and my heart was frantically beating. I was staring at her and thinking, *"Is this really happening?"* I wanted to reach out and help her but my legs were frozen in place.

My body was shivering uncontrollably and no matter how much I tried, I couldn't stop it. The next thing I knew I had been admitted to the hospital. The doctor put me on an IV and heavy-duty medication for three days to help my body stop shaking and get back to normal. I had experienced a nervous breakdown and was so out of it that when my little brother Roger came to visit me, I thought he had been gone for days when he would leave for a few minutes. Fortunately, while I was in the hospital, I found out my mother suffered only a few bruises and was fine. Amazingly, God had protected us from death a third time.

Hours after being discharged from the hospital, I was standing in a phone booth. As I told my sister in the U.S. what had happened, I broke out into a cold sweat and started to shake and shiver. The right side of my body became paralyzed, which prevented me from continuing to speak. Just by telling the story of the car bomb, I went into shock and ended up right back in the hospital. Slowly, I worked toward recovery. I knew that all I could do was to stay in the moment and do my best in order to *move forward…*

CHAPTER FIFTEEN

There's a Reason for Everything

In the midst of dealing with war and life's difficult challenges, I had the responsibility of staying mentally healthy for my daughter's sake. Fortunately, a ceasefire was soon declared. I used each one as an opportunity to go to the beach or mountains to take a deep breath like everyone else.

During one of those ceasefires, I met an interesting, kind man named Mike. At that point, my divorce was final and I was looking for a potential husband. He quickly won over my daughter's heart with his sweet actions. He seemed to be a true gentleman and was very persistent. Just like my mother had done with Sevag, she persuaded me to get to know him more.

"Aimmee, give him a chance," she said.

"I don't know him very well." I replied. "He seems very aggressive mom. I almost feel the same way I felt with Sevag. My intuition is telling me that something isn't right."

"You're feeling this way because you had a bad experience. Don't throw away your opportunity," she said. "You know how hard it is for a Lebanese woman in this day and age to find a man that will marry a divorced woman who has a daughter."

Mike put a smile on my face every time my daughter came in contact with him. He would often give her shoes from his family-owned shoe factory. Other gifts followed as well, always making her feel special. Mike knew that the best way to steal a woman's heart is to love her kids. I have to admit that he did an excellent job.

A month into my relationship, he took me to meet his family. Many of my other potential husbands wouldn't have done that considering I was a divorced, single mom.

Mike and I had two strong things in common. We had both lost dear loved ones in the war and had gone through a divorce. In an instant, he lost half of his family including his mother to a car bomb that destroyed several buildings. As a result, a lot of sadness and depression permeated his family. I connected with Mike on a deeper level than with Sevag since we both had lost loved ones in the war. I felt his deep pain and suffering.

Mike was admittedly wild and had sown his wild oats in his younger days before we met. I figured he was ready to settle down and enjoy family life. Another thing I liked was that he never treated me like I was second class, as other men of that day and time would have.

Having his family's support was also nice. They all loved me and my daughter, welcoming us both from the beginning. Back in those days in Middle Eastern culture, dating was not widely accepted unless a couple was engaged. Boyfriends had to be kept secret. Therefore, Mike and I couldn't just get to know each other and date without feeling uncomfortable. As a divorced woman, I was already judged. I knew the more time I spent with Mike, the more people would talk. I started feeling societal pressure.

When Mike asked for my hand in marriage, I was flattered. Before long, I also desperately wanted to give my daughter a normal family life with a father figure and stay-at-home mom. Although he was still grieving and wasn't working when we met, Mike promised that he would soon work with his father in the shoe factory. This would allow me to be home with my daughter. After all, he had made a special effort to be kind to her. Unlike many of the other men who wanted to date me, he never asked me to leave her behind with my family in order to marry me. With the hope of providing a better life for my daughter, I accepted Mike's marriage proposal.

At the time, mom was planning to return to Saudi Arabia and told us we could live in her apartment until she came back several months later. We were grateful for the offer as Mike was still living at home with his father, which was our tradition for unmarried sons. On the heels of mom's generous offer, we planned a small, simple wedding a couple weeks away.

In the meantime, my mom heard rumors that Mike had a serious anger management problem and a reputation for fighting, as a result of the tragedies he experienced with his family from the war. At the last minute, she tried to discourage me from marrying him, but it was too late. The wedding ceremony was already planned and paid for. Furthermore, his family and our guests had already been gearing up for the event and were very excited. Most importantly, I didn't want to disappoint my daughter, who by that time seemed to be enjoying the attention he gave her. I was *desperate* for my daughter to feel loved and accepted by a father figure.

Besides, Mike had never shown any signs of anger around me. This prompted me to give him the benefit of the doubt. I wanted to fit in and be normal, which meant having a husband. Back then, I was very insecure and struggling with my self worth, so I felt lucky to be accepted by him and his family. Above all, I wanted to give my daughter a better life, and I felt that I had finally found a potential husband and family who deeply cared about us.

Our wedding day was filled with love. His family did a wonderful job welcoming Silva and me into their lives. This was a sharp contrast from Sevag's family, who rejected me. Mike's family showered me with love and acceptance. It made me exceptionally happy.

Not even a week into the marriage, I discovered that Mike was numbing his severe pain with substances. This made him emotionally unstable and extremely edgy. At the time, we were taking my mom up on her generous offer and living at her place temporarily. Mike needed to start working so he could afford an apartment. Best of all, he didn't even need to look for a job. The job was already waiting for him.

"Mike, you promised us that you would work with your father soon after we got married," I said. "It has been two weeks already. When are you going to start?

"Don't ask any questions. It's none of your business when I start working!" he angrily responded.

Then, for the first time, he slapped me hard across the face. Just weeks into our marriage, whenever I was around him I was walking on eggshells. The smallest things could set him off. One time, I cooked meat a bit longer than he liked. Instantly, he became irate and threw his food across the room. I was absolutely shocked!

I wasn't expecting any of this. He wasn't the same person I'd met. It was obvious that he wasn't aware of his actions. Tragically, he was dealing with his painful grief in unhealthy ways and it was taking over his good, kind heart. Only weeks into my second marriage, I needed to find a solution. My intuition had been right after all.

Week by week, his behavior worsened. He began threatening me and it soon turned into hitting. Fortunately when he had his outbursts, Silva was at school or otherwise not around. I was so grateful for that.

With the pressure growing, my mind began racing with questions. *What am I going to do? If I leave him, how will I deal with my culture's belief system and judgement? Who am I to deserve more?* Sadly, I had no answers.

Feeling trapped and left with no choice, I started to convince myself that this was my fate, telling myself, "*Oh Aimmee, focus on the positive. Sure, he has anger issues, but he'll change one day. Just give him a chance. He has a good heart and loves you. On top of all that, his family accepts you and your daughter. What more can you ask for?*"

It was easier for me to *convince* myself than taking action. I went right back to the prison that I had created and hid in my shell. I began to blame everything that was happening in my life on the war again. If the war hadn't started, Robert would still be alive. He wouldn't allow anyone to treat me this way. The truth is that back then I couldn't find the *courage* to stand up for myself and do anything about my life.

*   *   *

Every once in a while my father would send money to help with Silva's school. When he did, the same conversation happened over and over.

"We need that money for living expenses," Mike would say.

"This money was sent for my daughter," I'd fearfully reply.

As usual, I did not want to make matters worse. *Stay in your shell and don't say anything Aimmee. Things will get better.* At least I thought. Sadly, his voice was more powerful than mine. Months passed and things only got worse.

One day, I finally found the courage to *speak up.* "I'm going to leave you if you're not going to stop acting like this," I said.

"What are you going to do?" he asked. "You don't have anywhere to go. What will people think of you if you get divorced again?"

Mike knew how to push the right buttons. He reminded me that Silva and I would be shunned by society if I left him. Adding to my dilemma, he knew that it would negatively affect my daughter's future.

Life with Mike was hard. He was extremely controlling and jealous. I remember one day when my family sent a package from Saudi Arabia through two Armenian gentlemen. Afraid that Mike might come home while they were there, I took the package from them at the door without inviting them in.

In Lebanon, if someone comes to your house to make a delivery, you are expected to invite them in for coffee and a snack. It is considered extremely rude not to offer. I felt horribly embarrassed for having to be discourteous and I tried to give the gentlemen a brief explanation. "I'm sorry, I can't let you in. My husband is coming home and he's not expecting to see anyone here."

Treating them that way really bothered me. They had gone out of their way to make the delivery. Acting that way was totally against our tradition too. Yet, my survival instinct had been engaged. When it came down to either being impolite to others or getting beaten by my husband, I unwillingly chose to be impolite.

Above all, the war would poke its giant head into the foreground. One day, while Mike was out, I was mopping the tile floor. I heard a bomb strike in the area. Immediately, I shifted into survival mode and got ready to head for safety in the basement. As I started to run, I slipped on the wet floor and jammed my foot on the edge of the door, splitting it between my big toe and the second. I ended up flat on my back in excruciating pain. It felt like my soul was coming out of my mouth. Meanwhile, the bombs kept coming. A second one and a third. I was unable to run for shelter due to my damaged foot and the paralyzing fear that had overcome me.

Finally, my neighbors found me and carried me off to safety. Later, I had my foot examined by a physician. When I told him I was twenty-four, he told me it would take one day for every year of my life for my foot to heal to the point where I could walk. He was right. Twenty four days later, I was able to walk, but unfortunately I was unable to walk away from Mike.

I had no idea how to get out of that situation. I couldn't move without his permission. He became completely obsessed with me and controlled me by attacking my weak spots. All of these actions came from his fear of losing me.

"You need to send your daughter away to her family," he said one day.

"You know that's not possible. She is everything to me," I replied.

As Mike was trying to cope with his many losses, his anger grew stronger. I sympathized with his pain. We both had experienced many tragedies due to the war. Trying to cope with his emotional issues made it hard for me to handle my own. Dealing with his personal turmoil placed an even heavier load on my shoulders. It was difficult trying to comfort him when I needed someone to comfort me.

After every time Mike hit me, he would give me what seemed to be a genuine, heartfelt apology. He was amazingly convincing and I'd believe him when he'd say he'd never do it again, not knowing that I was making a *choice*. It was as if he didn't want to abuse me, but he just couldn't help himself.

That was a very dark period of time for me. My daughter was the life force that kept me going. Without her, I wouldn't have been able to even get up in the morning. I would do anything for her. God gave her to me for a reason. When she was in a deep sleep, she looked like an angel. I would lie next to her and felt I had everything I needed. I wanted to give her everything and those precious moments kept my batteries charged. I had to keep going for her.

*　　*　　*

One Sunday, while most families were enjoying fun summertime outings, Mike and I were fighting. For the first and only time, he hit me in front of my nine year old daughter. He completely lost it and started beating me so badly that I yelled to Silva to call for help. She searched up and down the building looking for someone we knew. Unable to find anybody home, she quickly ran back into our apartment in a total panic. When I saw the fear in my daughter's eyes, I somehow found *courage*. Mike was hitting me hard, but seeing my daughter witnessing her mother being beaten was harder. Then and there, I decided that I didn't want Mike in my life anymore.

Soon, some neighbors returned home and with them standing by, I put his clothes by the door to let him know that I wanted him to leave. By then, Mike had calmed down from his rage, having made the abrupt switch to his apologetic side. He didn't resist and thought that the whole thing would blow over and I would soon calm down, like I always had. However, this time I was serious. He had hit me in front of my daughter and I was not going to accept that.

I looked Mike in the eye and told him that he wasn't going to hit me in front of her ever again. After that, we separated and Mike went back home to live with his family.

Once again, I had to figure out how I was going to face society, deal with their belief system, and make it alone as a single mother. As you know, I also needed to find work but didn't fit the profile that employers were looking for.

A great opportunity was soon dropped in my lap by a friend. "Aimmee, I have an idea for you," she said. "Your uncle owns a store. Unfortunately, he isn't well right now. Why don't you take over his place and turn it into a costume jewelry shop? I know some vendors who will supply you with the product. You don't have to pay them until you sell the merchandise. You're an elegant young lady, and many people would love to buy from you!"

"Yes! Of course I will. I would love to do that," I enthusiastically replied. "Wow, that is awesome!"

I was so excited and optimistic about this. In the back of my mind, I started planning. I thought about the store layout, how easy it was going to be to have my own store, and where I could hire someone who would do the things that I couldn't do, such as reading and writing. I knew that would give me the freedom to focus on customers and make business decisions.

I quickly went to my uncle and approached him with the idea. "Yes, of course you can," he said. "Would you work with me on the rent?"

"Yes, I would love to help you out," I said. "Thank you so much!" I walked away filled with hope and a new vision for my future.

Shortly after I left, my uncle contacted my mom. When I walked into our apartment, mom was on the phone with him saying that she didn't support my business idea.

"If she couldn't handle school, how is she going to handle the business? Aimmee would probably turn the business into a disaster and fail, just like she did with school," mom told him.

Losing that opportunity deeply hurt. It didn't help my self esteem either. What was I going to do now?

I still remember how I dealt with that situation. I went out to the balcony and looked up to the sky. I was overwhelmed and desperate for *hope*. Slowly, I started feeling resentment and anger toward my mom. *Oh no God. This is not a good feeling. I don't want to go there. I need to stop NOW!* Then, I slowly took several deep breaths, and called upon my imaginary best friend whom I hadn't reached out to in a long time. What I heard was very *simple* but powerful. *"Aimmee, in order to keep peace in your heart and mind, you must believe that what happened has nothing to do with you or your mom. Having your own store is not meant to be for you right now. In your heart, you know that everything happens for a reason. You must continue to believe that."* I went back into the living room with a fresh, new outlook of the situation.

Today, I know without a doubt that everything happens for a reason. If I had become the owner of that store, it would have been a success, because years later, I discovered that one of my strengths is being an entrepreneur. However, if that would have happened, this book would have never been written and I wouldn't be living my true purpose right now.

* * *

Years earlier, I had been approached many times to work as a belly dancer, but always refused the offers. Around the time of my separation with Mike, I was asked again.

Back in those days, most people did not view belly dancing as art or as a decent job. Even though it was my reputation, I knew that it would affect my daughter's future. Therefore, I always did my absolute best to keep my reputation solid. However, now I was *desperate*. The reality is that I couldn't find anything else. I needed to put food on the table and felt I had no other choice than to take what was in front of me. Although I had always been a gifted dancer, it wasn't what I wanted to do for a living. Like the acting jobs, dancing required some travel. Having to be away from my daughter made me feel like I had gone back to square one. The separation from Mike completely destroyed my hope of having a normal family.

Before long, I heard rumors that Mike wanted to work things out. When I heard this, I was thrilled. The thought of having family again was so exciting. I really wanted to believe it. We soon started talking again.

"I want to get back together and make things right with you Aimmee. I promise that I will not hit you again. To prove to you that I'm serious, I already started working with my father. You can ask him to see for yourself," he humbly said.

"Yes, of course. I will do my best to work things out," I happily replied, feeling that my prayers had been answered. I had always liked his good side and he seemed sincere. We decided to try again.

Around that time, I had to take another trip for work. I really didn't want to go, but we felt that the money I'd earn would help us get on our feet without help from our families. Mike's income wasn't enough to pay for rent, causing me to look for work. The plan for my work trip was that I would stay for a month. However, within a few days of being there, I started having anxiety attacks and my blood pressure plummeted due to the stress and missing my daughter. I had no choice and terminated my contract early and return to Lebanon. Even though the job didn't work out, I grew excited about a new idea I had.

Upon my return, I convinced Mike to seek work in Saudi Arabia. "Jobs are plentiful there," I told him. "I'll be close to my family and we'd get away from the war."

He thought it was a great idea. "Yes, let's do it," he enthusiastically responded. We quickly got our belongings together and flew to Jeddah, a major Saudi port.

My father and my brother Jack greeted us at the airport. That was the first time Mike met the rest of my family. It meant the world for dad to see me due to his declining health and his need for something that would lift his spirits. Upon our arrival, Silva was immensely glad to see her grandpa. She ran to hug him. He picked her up, even though he probably shouldn't have, considering his health. Silva and my dad were very close. He would put her on his lap and give her the fatherly attention she craved.

Unfortunately, dad had caught wind of the problems Mike and I had been facing. Signs of concern showed through his eyes. Yet, he was a very diplomatic man and didn't interfere in our relationship. It meant a lot when my dad said he trusted me to make good decisions.

A few years earlier, my parents became born again Christians and their marital relationship turned around. After God came into my dad's life, whenever I'd talk to him, he'd pray for me and his prayers helped to lift my spirits. As a result, my relationship with God grew deeper and stronger too, which helped me cope with the difficulties of my day-to-day life.

During that visit, my father noticed that Silva seemed hungrier than usual for attention. I agreed that she was in special need of fatherly attention, a role which Mike was sadly not fulfilling.

While we were in Saudi Arabia, my grandma in Lebanon passed away. I was glad I wasn't there. Burying grandma would have been difficult.

All my good memories of her came back in a flash; the tick tock of her grandfather clock, taking naps on her sofa, and feeling safe. I remembered how I used to go to her house when I was little and how she would prepare wonderful home-cooked meals. Her house was always peaceful and it was one of the only places where I felt like I could be a child. Grandma would often do special things for me when I'd visit. She would cook my favorite dish kibbee. Above all, she made me feel loved and protected. Not attending the funeral helped me keep these loving and caring memories alive.

*   *   *

Things didn't work out for us in Saudi Arabia. Despite Mike trying to find a job, he couldn't get the proper work permits. Before long, it was clear to us that we had to return to Beirut. The night before we left, the entire family came together and had dinner. It was a wonderful blessing to have everyone together. Dad teared up as he looked around the table at his loved ones. He said a prayer and then we enjoyed our meal.

The next morning, we packed our bags and began saying our goodbyes as taxi soon arrived. My brother and Mike were loading the luggage in the trunk as I stood on the balcony saying goodbye to my father. He asked me to give him a hug. The way he said it suggested that it might be the last embrace I'd ever give him. Around that time, my father desperately needed to have heart surgery. However, he refused to undergo the operation. He didn't want to take the risk until he was sure that his family would be well taken care of. We both had tears in our eyes as we said goodbye. While we hugged, I felt like I wanted to hang on to him forever, but I knew I had to leave.

*　　*　　*

It didn't take long for Mike to return to his old habits after we returned to Lebanon. He was disappointed that he was unable to find work in Saudi Arabia. Like any man in his situation, he felt highly discouraged and frustrated.

I still hoped Mike would go back to work in his family's business. Besides improving our quality of life with the income, I thought maybe if he started working, it would cheer him up. Every night I would pray to God, asking Him to help Mike find peace. Although he was in denial, I felt sorry for him and empathized with his pain. I had always known that deep down he had a kind heart, but he felt showing it would be a sign of weakness.

Mike soon started working in his dad's company. Regrettably, his job there was short-lived and he quickly lost his opportunity. Being the owner's son, he naturally expected special treatment. However, his dad was not about to go along with that and refused to allow him to show up late. He knew that if he treated his son differently that the other employees would have gotten disgruntled. In addition, Mike didn't take the job seriously. How he coped with his pain caused him to be irritable and irresponsible, which caused a rift between him and his father in the work place. Outside of work though, the two of them got along fine.

Meanwhile, my dad was busy helping Jacque in Saudi Arabia and started to make a better living. With the extra money, he retired my mother and sent her to Lebanon with the down payment for a new apartment. Under Middle Eastern tradition, parents who could afford it would buy houses for their male children. That way, when they got married they would have a place to take their wives. Similarly, parents stay involved with their children throughout their lives, helping them to find jobs and even spouses.

Now that my mom was back in Beirut, she wanted her old apartment, which is where Mike and I were living. Having her things there, along with neighbors she liked, made it convenient. We had nowhere else to go, so mom graciously offered to let us use her new apartment until we got on our feet. I didn't want my daughter to witness Mike's increasingly furious behavior or to feel rejected, so I made the tough decision for her to live with my mom for several months for her protection. Even though the apartments were a block from each other and I got to see Silva almost daily, I still greatly missed having her with me all the time. I chose to miss her, knowing she'd be safe, instead of having her stay with me noticing that she was unwanted by Mike.

I used to cry myself to sleep. I got married to give her a family, yet ended up having to send her away instead. I stayed in that bad marriage, believing that it would be better for Silva to have a battered mom, instead of a twice divorced one in our culture. I figured I could always disguise the bruises.

On the other hand, I wanted to get out of that situation, but had no money or ideas of what to do. I prayed and asked God for help. He gave me his answer through a neighbor. Her family was moving to the United States. Due to the fact I had one more month left on my visa, she suggested that I go there too. I felt that God was sending me a message and I was determined to heed it. I had this distinct feeling that things would work out this time.

I talked to Mike about going and he loved the idea too. We would have nothing to lose. "Let's give it a shot," he said. I could see that he was looking forward to leaving his bad memories behind, and starting a new life! I started seeing the opportunity and feeling *hope*.

Unlike the U.S., there were two major things working against me in Lebanon. The first was the culture's belief system. In order to be an entrepreneur and have business opportunities, you had to have a solid education or to have been born into an influential family. The second obstacle was the suffering government. Since the war had understandably crippled the Lebanese government, the quality of life was at a severe low. There was no police station to call and nobody to reach out to for help. The country was not stable. Each person was on his or her own. I was not able to live a full, healthy life. We were all paying a high price due to the war. The stability and freedom of the U.S. would allow me to live a lifestyle that I always dreamed of for me and my daughter.

As I look back now, I can see that there was another thing stopping me. The third and most powerful obstacle was my own personal belief system about myself. The truth of the matter is that I was in my own way. Deep down, I knew I could change my life but my beliefs about myself prevented me from doing so. I chose to ignore that I had the power to change my life.

I imagined how life would be different in the U.S. Mike would no longer be able to rely financially on his family or mine. He would definitely have to work. I knew he would be cautious about losing his temper since the U.S. had a strong police presence. Our lives were definitely going to change.

Meanwhile, Silva was regularly visiting Sevag's family. They were encouraging her to visit her father in the U.S., telling her about how beautiful the schools and parks were, and how she could visit Disneyland again.

Her strong desire to visit the U.S. and see her father was something I'd never seen in her before. It was another message from God telling me that I should take action. Deep in my heart, I knew that this time I was traveling for a very *good* reason. *If I move to the U.S., I'll be close to my daughter when she visits her father. She'll also be away from the war and safe.* That was a very powerful motive to do whatever it took in my power to make things happen. After all, she was my *why*. She lifted me up when I needed it the most and kept me going every day.

Mike didn't have a visa yet, so he let us leave without him before ours expired. He planned to follow as soon as he got the stamp of approval. We hardly had a penny to our names. Thankfully, God provided a way for us to get the tickets. I sold furniture to pay for mine. Sevag's family agreed to pay for Silva's, and Mike's family lent him the money for his. A good lifelong friend of mine, Ghada, who was once Kani's best friend, bought a TV from me that she didn't really need, just to help me get the funds together.

As Silva and I boarded the plane for America for the third time, I was hopeful of what the future held. At the same time, with Mike soon to follow, I wasn't sure what was going to happen. Though I loved Lebanon, my beautiful country with its mild weather, cedar-topped mountains, and blue ocean, I knew I would not be coming back for a long time.

Like a puzzle, all of the pieces were starting to come together for a reason . . .

CHAPTER SIXTEEN

Keeping Hope Alive

With one week left on my visa in 1988, my daughter and I flew to the U.S. for the third time. We landed at the airport in Orlando, Florida. I was optimistic and felt hope and a sense of peace in my heart. This time, I was determined to stay and make it work regardless of the cost.

We stayed with my sister for a few weeks while waiting for Mike to arrive. In the meantime, I started to make arrangements with Sevag for Silva to visit him in Hawaii. He had been living there for several years with his girlfriend and her two daughters, who were both around Silva's age. Knowing that she'd be living with a woman with kids made me feel comfortable. My little girl was at a tender age and I knew his girlfriend would be able to take care of her.

Within a few days, we received a plane ticket for Silva from her dad. Although I was happy for her to have this opportunity, the thought of her leaving was heartbreaking. As you know by now, she was my everything.

When we were saying our goodbyes at the airport, I got on my knees and hugged her, pulling her close to my heart. I didn't want to let her go. However, despite my motherly instincts, I had to do what was best for her, as I usually did. In order to let her go with ease, I convinced myself that her dad had a stable job and would be able to help her become a

U.S. citizen. While watching her plane take off, I felt more determined than ever to do whatever it would take to bring her back.

A few weeks after Silva left, Mike arrived in Florida and joined me at my sister's house. It didn't take long before we realized that we couldn't make it work there. We sat down and talked about our options. I had some relatives on my father's side and Mike had a few close friends in Los Angeles. There was also a large Middle Eastern community there. All of those facts made it clear to us that moving to L.A. was the best decision.

*   *   *

We arrived at the Los Angeles International Airport with high expectations and excitement. My father's side of the family welcomed us. Even though we were not close, they gave us the opportunity to stay with them for a couple of days. It was a chance for us to take a deep breath and plan our next step. I was grateful for the shelter, but it was hard dealing with my family because they had all heard about Mike's temper and the marital problems we had experienced back in Lebanon. Even though my father had always spoken highly of me, my relatives didn't know me well. They didn't know what to think of me based on what they had heard about Mike. Naturally, my relatives had their own lives and rightfully didn't want to get bogged down with my problems. Who would blame them?

After a few days of staying with my relatives, longtime friends of Mike's, Jack and his wife Suzanne, took us in with open arms. We stayed with them for a couple of weeks while we searched for work. Jack introduced us to his friend Sako and his wife. They were a nice Armenian couple with two kids who welcomed us into their home even though we were strangers.

Sako found jobs for us with his friend Nebil, a nice Palestinian Muslim gentleman who was married with two kids and managed a bakery. He and his wife were kind people who went out of their way to help us get on our feet. To make it easier for us to get to work, Nebil and his family opened up their home to us so that we could catch a ride to work with him. They didn't have a spare bedroom, but out of the goodness of their hearts, they inconvenienced themselves and made a way for us to sleep in their living room. They chose to rise above their personal and religious beliefs and do the right thing. In Lebanon, the Muslims and Christians were in a war with each other. Yet, here we were in a foreign country helping one another.

Even though I was grateful for help from Nebil and his family, I was constantly thinking and worrying about my daughter. *What is she doing now? Is she eating well? Is she doing her homework?* Endless questions stirred in my mind. I also missed my family so much, especially my dad.

Mike felt stuck and unhappy, which only made him harder to live with. Living in someone else's home was something we appreciated, but being a married couple without your own place felt like a burden. I lived one day at a time trying to hold on to my dream of a better tomorrow. My why is what kept me going and I was determined to persevere.

With Nebil's assistance, Mike and I were able to save some money. After living with him and his family for about three weeks, we rented a tiny studio apartment. Nebil helped us clean it up and gave us some furniture. The studio was a couple of blocks away from his house, so he continued to drive us to work each week to help us save a bit more. Soon, we bought a secondhand car and started driving ourselves to work. I was very grateful. I told myself that my marriage would be better once we had our own place.

Mike thought that he'd be able to leave his painful war memories behind. He didn't realize that he was still grieving and struggling with the loss of his mother. Until he dealt with those issues, he would not have been happy no matter where he went or what he did. Unable to get away from the reality, his desire to return to Lebanon grew stronger. The war had successfully stolen his happiness and soul.

*   *   *

Every couple of weeks or so, I spoke to my dad on the phone. Simply hearing his voice was comforting and helped me get through that dark period. Around that time, he made arrangements to visit the U.S. on business. He was doing fairly well with his inventions and arranged a meeting with some potential investors to present an antipollution device he had developed for cars. When he told me his plans, I was ecstatic and reminded him about what he said in Saudi Arabia. "See dad, you shouldn't have said goodbye. We will get to see each other again. I can't wait to see you."

Things got particularly strained between Mike and me during a time when I hadn't heard from my father for about a month. I was worried every day that something had happened to him. My dad always made a point to stay in touch with me in an effort to lift my spirits and I desperately wanted to talk to him. *Why is he not calling? Is he okay?* I knew my dad had been ill and needed to have heart surgery. I prayed to God every moment, *"Please God, keep my father safe. I need him more than ever!*

One day, while looking forward to my dad's upcoming arrival, Mike answered the phone. As he spoke to the caller, he shook his head in despair. Out of frustration and disappointment, he hit the wall with his fist Mike didn't say anything, but the disturbed look on his face said it all. I immediately knew something had happened to my father.

"Oh God! No! Please God! No!" I cried out. Shocked and in disbelief, I kept repeating "Please God! No! Why now? Why? You're being too hard on me!" I shrieked in despair and felt like my heart and soul had been ripped out of my chest. Any happiness and hope in my heart vanished. I dropped to the floor and balled myself up into a fetal position, weeping quietly. Since my childhood days, my dad had been the most influential person to me on this earth. He was in his early 60s when he passed away. I wished someone from my family was there with me.

I desperately needed and wanted to hug my daughter. There was a special strength and comfort that I only received from her. As I cried, I wondered how I was going to tell her the news, especially with her being so far away. I had no doubt in my heart and mind that she would feel the same. If she knew about her grandpa's death, she would want me to hug her and let her cry on my shoulders.

Silva overheard that something had happened to her grandpa from her dad and sensed that something was wrong. During one of our phone conversations, she kept asking about her grandpa over and over.

"Tell me what's happened to him," she said. "Don't hide it from me, mom." She pressed on saying, "I haven't heard from grandpa in a while. Can you tell him to call me?"

Now she had me on the spot and I couldn't avoid answering her honest question. Hearing her words made me break down, and I finally gave in and told her that he passed away. Unable to speak another word, she simply hung up the phone. In that moment, I wished I could fly like a bird and reach out to her. Unfortunately, she had to face this reality without her mother.

As I grieved the loss of my beloved father, I felt like all the doors in my life were closing in every direction. Mike's unhappiness was still a daily obstacle. Living so far away from my eleven-year-old daughter was weighing heavily on my heart.

Likewise, life threw Sevag a difficult curveball as well. He came home one day to discover that his girlfriend had packed up and left without warning, just like I did when she and I visited him several years earlier. Understandably, he was emotionally distraught. Consequently, he couldn't be there to comfort Silva with her grief, since he was caught up with his own emotional turmoil.

Things didn't get any better. Around that time, Silva's other grandpa passed away. I had known him since I was fourteen years old and he had consistently treated me with kindness. Dealing with his death was hard. By the age of twenty six, I had lost eleven family members.

As a result, Silva was forced to deal with the deaths of her grandfathers by herself. Even though we were miles apart, I felt every second of her pain.

Fear of the unknown sank in. *How is my daughter dealing with her grief? How can she handle all of this by herself?* The only thing I could do for her at that moment was to stay strong. I was *not* going to allow anything to break me down. *Not now! Not ever!* I needed to *fight* for our lives.

Every single night, I made sure to take a moment to meditate and pray. I would cover myself up with the bed's sheet and tell myself, *"Calm down Aimmee. This is the time I need to connect with my soul. Let go of everything. Just breathe in and out slowly."* I would repeat the breathing at least ten times until I was able to hear and *feel* my heartbeat. Then, I would ask for guidance and support. Every time I did that, I heard the same answer, *"Aimmee, turn your fear into faith."* Doing so helped me see the light during those dark days.

One of Sevag's friends soon reached out to my daughter. She was a kind Middle Eastern woman named Mona. While Sevag was at work, she watched Silva and comforted her when no one else was around. I would talk to Mona every chance I had. Knowing that Silva was in good hands and being cared for brought me great comfort and relief. My prayer had been answered through Mona and I was deeply grateful for her caring heart.

Without Sevag's former girlfriend around, the responsibility of raising Silva was getting harder for him. He soon decided to have her live with Mike and me in L.A. At that time, we were struggling and living in a tiny, single room. Our place was too small for all three of us to live there. Regardless of the limitations or any obstacles, I was thrilled knowing I'd have my daughter back with me. I counted down every day, every moment, and every second, anxiously waiting for her to arrive.

*   *   *

Having Silva back and living in a small place made Mike more uptight. He felt more responsibility and pressure. This only served to make him more unhappy.

"We need to go back to Lebanon," Mike would say, on a regular basis. "I can't handle living in the United States. If I get injured or fired from my job, we will definitely be homeless. Everyone we know has helped us as much as they can. This is not our place. We need to leave."

"This time I'm not leaving," I would continually tell him. "I'd rather be homeless than live in the midst of war, running around from place to place and waking up in the middle of the night not knowing if we'd survive. The war has successfully destroyed both of our families' lives."

Mike couldn't deny that I was speaking the truth.

I continued on, "I am not going to allow the war to steal my daughter's life. This is my opportunity to give her a better life, away from the fear of war and the unknown. I'm going to fight to the last minute I have on this earth in order to keep us both safe and sound."

There is definitely a reason I had to come back to this country for the third time. I was determined to stay.

He would always be shocked and surprised every time I refused to give in and leave the country.

As he would tightly hold me by my arm, he would angrily say, "So what are you going to do now? Do you want to get divorced again? Is that what you want? Answer me! You can't answer me because you know what would happen to you. You will have no future, you or your daughter. Being divorced twice will definitely make your family ashamed of you. People will look at you like you're an outcast, and not able to keep your family together. No one is going to help you. If you decide to stay here, you're going to find yourself in a foreign country and all alone."

Over the next several months, tension continued to escalate between Mike and me. He was condescending and constantly wanting to start another argument. The war had damaged Mike in so many different ways. He lost his family, along with his kind heart and soul. In the process, he also lost his ability to be in control of his emotions, as was common with many people who go through horrific war trauma.

* * *

One day while Silva was at school, I prepared lunch for Mike as usual. I had everything ready just the way he liked, but I had forgotten to put the vegetables on the table.

"Where are the vegetables?" he demanded, as he sat down to eat. I could tell that he was about to lose his temper.

"Oh, I'm sorry. I forgot to put them out," I said peacefully. I got up to get them, hoping that he'd calm down. "They're already prepared. They're in the refrigerator."

"What do you mean you left them in the refrigerator?" he screamed, as he flipped the table upside down. Then he threw a block of cheese which hit me right on the side of the face. That blow aggravated my tooth that had been sore for months and already painful.

Right then, I decided that I had gone through enough. I no longer cared what people would think of me if I got divorced a second time.

"That's it!" I told him. "I'll go through any obstacle, whether it's being an outcast or being homeless before I stay with you any longer!"

By that time, he had calmed down from his rage and started to be humble and apologetic. He asked for forgiveness.

"I promise on my mom's grave that I will never hit you again," he sorrowfully said.

He thought that maybe I'd change my mind about leaving him, as I had always done before. It was one of the most difficult things to deal with. I was only in my early twenties, and as you know I had been through many difficult situations.

"I can't do this anymore," I said firmly.

In my heart, I knew that I tried everything in my power to keep my marriage. I had hoped to stand by my troubled husband. He was riding an emotional roller coaster and was grieving the loss of most of his family. However, the price of staying with Mike had became far too high.

After several days of heartfelt discussions, Mike and I agreed to sign a separation agreement. We both knew that it was the right thing to do for everyone's sake. Later on, our divorce was finalized. Like other victims of war, the emotional turmoil had left its mark.

*   *   *

I was afraid of moving on, but I wasn't confused on where I wanted to be in life. I took the first step towards taking action. As usual, I turned my fear *into faith*, asking myself, *"Do I want to be the victim? Or do I want to be the victor?"*

I packed our clothes and walked away not knowing what was going to happen. The only person who had helped and guided me through difficult situations had always been my dad, and now he was gone. *How I am going to make it with no support system? How I am going to survive?*

Many people told me, "Go back to your country. You can't make it here on your own."

Their words brought difficult questions to my mind. *Should I give in? Should I stand up and fight?* The answer was crystal clear. I knew deep in my heart that I had my *why*, my daughter. I knew she would help me keep my head *high* and find my way. This was my opportunity to make something of my life and I was determined.

It was 1989 when I was on my own again as a single mother. This time, it was in a new country with no home to go to. I didn't have a job or speak the language. All I had was a few hundred dollars in my pocket. Despite the odds, I kept my hope alive and found the courage to walk away from my troubled marriage and start a *new* life.

That was the end of the first chapter of my life and the beginning of the *next*.

CHAPTER SEVENTEEN

Rising Above and Living
the American Dream

Sharing the details of my life's second chapter would require me to write another book. It would be a story with severe lows and incredible highs, perseverance and persistence, lessons and personal growth, and best of all, proud moments filled with *hope*! However, I would like to share a couple of the *proudest* moments with you.

In the early 90s, I married a wonderful man who dearly loved me and cared for my daughter who still stands behind me to this day. Several years into my marriage, I became an entrepreneur. Later on, Silva got married.

At the age of 32, I was overjoyed to welcome my first grandson, Steven, who was followed by another grandson, Sovante and two beautiful granddaughters, Kasandra and Izel of whom I feel like they are gifts from God.

One of the most beautiful experiences was seeing my daughter dressed in her blue cap and gown, walking across the stage at her college graduation to receive her nursing degree.

Fast forward to 2005. Exactly thirty years after the horrible war tragedy that claimed my brother Robert's life, I had just finished a successful business meeting.

As I proudly walked toward my car, I was gushing with excitement and delight. I felt alive for the first time in years. I got in the car and inserted a CD by one of my favorite singers, Celine Dion. I rolled down the window, looked up at the beautiful sky and took a couple of deep breaths. Then, I turned my car on and started driving down the freeway.

All of a sudden, memories from childhood through adulthood started to flash back. It was like a movie trailer in my mind. I felt as if I were living my life all over again. You can only imagine how overwhelmed I was. Mixed emotions took over my body.

As I was distracted by my feelings and thoughts, cars started honking. Drivers began shouting and waving their hands. They yelled, "Hey! Come on! Go faster!" Quickly, I realized that I was holding up traffic. In that moment, I knew that I needed to stop driving. I took the first exit I saw and pulled over in a large desert area.

As I turned off my car, I put my head on the steering wheel and broke down crying. Tears were running down my face. Fortunately, those tears were *tears of joy, appreciation and disbelief.*

Years ago, I had been a woman with no hope or opportunity. Now, I had been given the freedom and the right to raise my voice and stand up for myself.

Next, something magical happened. For a moment, I felt like I was in a dream. I heard my own voice say, *"It's time to share your story."*

As I came back to reality, I felt like my thoughts were running through every inch of my body. I told myself, *"Absolutely not! That's not going to happen. I'm a private person and I want to keep it that way. Why would I even want to do such a thing?"*

I heard the answer strongly. *"You must put your interest on the side and do what you're here to do."*

I was going back and forth in my mind, as the doubts wouldn't seem to let go.

"Who is going to care about what I have to share?" I thought. *"Most importantly, how am I going to tell my story to the world?*

However, the intuitive urge to share my story was overwhelmingly powerful. I knew what I had to do. I raised my head back up, took one deep breath, looked at the sky, and asked myself the most important question. *Should I listen to my mind and be logical, or follow my heart and be guided?* I didn't hear an answer, but my body automatically took action and I turned the car back on.

My mind was in complete silence. For the first time in my life, I could feel my heart beat and hear every breath I was taking without going in a meditative state. It felt like I was in a different world and I wasn't in control of my body. The whole experience was surreal.

Somehow, I made it back home. My husband wasn't feeling well that day so he was at the house resting, watching television and reading the newspaper.

As I walked into the family room where he was, he looked at me and asked, "What's wrong? Are you okay? It looks like you've been crying."

"Nothing to worry about," I calmly answered. "I am doing fine."

"I can tell that something is wrong. What happened?" he continued.

I gave in and told him.

"Okay," he responded. "What are you going to do about it?"

"Well," I said. "I am going to write my story."

He went silent, allowing my words to sink in.

A few moments later, he said, "You've surprised me many times. I know how smart you are and I know you're capable of running a business and dealing with life's obstacles and challenges. However, doing that is one thing. Writing a book is another. The other thing is that you're a very private person. Do you really want everyone to know the intimate details of your life?"

It was clear to me that he was looking out for my best interest. He meant well with his words and was speaking the truth.

"How are you going to do all that?," he asked. "How are you going to write a book when you only have a fourth grade education and you've never read a book in your life?"

My answer was simple. "As long I have my *why*, the *how* will appear."

*   *   *

I walked away towards my home office. Sitting in my comfortable rocking chair, I looked up to the ceiling. All I could think about was why my life was saved. When the first bomb hit our apartment in 1975, it should have been me who died instead of Robert. As you know, I was originally going to stay in the living room and Robert was going to get his tea. Now, not only was I alive and living in the most powerful country in the world, but I was also living the American dream. Here, I could be whoever I wanted to be . . . even an author with a fourth grade education. In that moment, I realized that everything I had endured had led me here and that it was not a coincidence.

I felt compelled to share my story. I wanted to help other people see their lives in a different perspective and to know that they're not alone. It was my time to pay it forward. I completely stopped thinking about *how* I was going to write the book. Instead, I allowed myself to listen to my heart and surrender to being guided. While I was praying, I was able to fully feel, breathe in the present moment and live in the now.

Writing and personally publishing the first edition of *Tears of Hope* was not an easy task. Reliving the unpleasant memories of my life was extremely painful. Creating the book helped me uncover even more powerful lessons. One of them is that forgiving doesn't mean forgetting. Our life story is part of us just like our fingerprint.

A year and a half later, the first edition of *Tears of Hope* was born. When I received my copy, I felt like I was holding a newborn baby who needed my attention, love and patience. I felt proud that I had followed my intuition and had stepped into taking action. All of it brought me joy, excitement and happiness. Yet, a huge question remained . . . Am I *completely* satisfied with my book? Every time I asked myself that question, the answer came from the readers. I received many testimonials on how *Tears of Hope* helped them see their life in different perspective. Each time I read someone's testimonial, I felt compelled to continue on this ever-unfolding journey.

Although I personally grew and evolved with the first edition of *Tears of Hope*, I experienced many sleepless nights for seven years. Even though I had followed my intuition and understood the reason why I wrote my book, deep in my soul, I knew that I was not completely stepping into my light. Something was missing. From time to time I heard my inner voice saying, *"Aimmee, you need to rewrite the book and share your true message."* Every time I heard those haunting words, I took my book, ran away and hid in my shell. I ignored the truth and held on to it like a child in a mother's hands.

Every time I was signing or giving my book away, I felt extremely uncomfortable deep in my core. I knew that the true message was not part of the book. I kept ignoring my inner voice and convinced myself not to move on or do anything about it. This continued for several years. I kept telling myself that I wasn't ready for the task. Living my true purpose would come with great responsibility and unwavering commitment.

In the meantime, I continued doing radio interviews, speaking, coaching and seminars. That's where I felt the most comfortable. Through each of those activities, I witnessed people open their minds, hearts and souls. I literally could see and feel the happiness on their faces as they stepped into their *light* and started living their purpose. It was extremely humbling to experience such blessings. Here I was living my purpose. What more could I ask for? My inner voice came back to haunt me once again, saying *"You're not done yet."*

The only response I could offer was, "What do you mean I'm not done yet? I'm doing everything I can to help people see their light." My inner voice continued, "Yes, you're on the right track. The more people you help, the more help you're going to receive. You're going to be surprised about how many of them step in and help you with your mission. Aimmee, your life was saved for reason. You found a way to find peace in your heart and stay in the light. Now, you must share your gift with the world and live your true purpose."

I let the words sink deep into my soul, and heard more. "Your true purpose is to help humanity and be the voice for victims of war and people who lost their dreams, hope, and souls. Your life is about helping others find peace in their hearts and minds so they can stay in their light and make a difference in the world."

Those words were powerful, yet for years I went back and forth. I persisted at ignoring my inner voice. However, deep in my soul, I knew that I was running away from the responsibility of stepping up and living my true purpose. Like a little girl, I would run away and hide in my shell. I felt the most comfortable there, like most of us do. I continued convincing myself that I was living my purpose and I don't need to do anything else.

It was 2005 when I started writing the first edition of *Tears of Hope*. In 2010, I could no longer ignore my inner voice. From that moment on, I made the decision to listen to God and allow him to guide me and help me in completely stepping into my light and living my true purpose. I opened my mind, heart and soul, to taking small steps towards writing *Tears of Hope*, expanding on and sharing more of my insights.

It took me over two years to slowly allow myself to come out of my shell and finish this new edition of *Tears of Hope*. This time, I was ready and open to share my message. In November of 2012 I found a publisher who believed in me and was willing to help me share my message with the world.

*   *   *

I believe we all live under one light. No matter who you are or where you come from, we all have the opportunity to bond and lift each other up so we all can shine. Remember earlier when I heard my inner voice telling me about the people who were going to step in and help me share my message? I soon discovered that it truly was a direct message from God. Here's proof of one of the angels who showed up to further my mission.

It all began when I was conducting one of my seminars in 2012. A good friend of mine, Liz Nitta, was helping me organize the event. Liz recommended my seminar to a friend and client of hers, named Stephanie Thompson. Stephanie did not know what to expect from my seminar. You could tell she was not that excited about being there.

However, within the first ten minutes, Stephanie was lighting up. Since that day, Stephanie started to see her life and light in a different perspective. She went home excited about life. Perhaps she can share her own testimonial with you at a different time.

A couple of days later, Stephanie called me and asked me if I would be interested in coaching her. I replied, "Yes, of course. I'd love to do that."

She was happy when she heard my answer. "As you know, I am a singer and actor," she said. "Aimmee, I would love for you to hear my voice so you can have an idea about some of what I do."

"Of course, I'd love to hear your voice," I simply replied.

Just like her when she came to my seminar, I had no idea what to expect. I sat comfortably on the stool waiting patiently for her to set up and start singing. It took her ten minutes when she started to see the light in my seminar. It took me ten seconds to see and hear her talents. It was one of the most unbelievable, powerful and incredible voices that I personally had ever heard! From that moment on, I knew in my heart that I was going to do everything I could to help her shine and guide her to live her true purpose.

A month or so into my coaching, Stephanie called. "Aimmee, I have been wanting to show my appreciation and do something special for you. I appreciate you and admire you so much. I decided to tell your story through a song as a gift from me."

She began sharing the lyrics with me. I must say that I was so impressed, but not surprised. She brought tears of joy to my eyes. It was a humbling experience to see someone appreciating what I do.

Two weeks later, I was in my kitchen preparing food for my husband, when I sensed light surrounding me and I heard my inner voice saying, *"You must ask Stephanie to help you write a song about peace in the world. The song must be about that twelve year old little girl named Aimmee. That little girl's life was saved for a reason. It is about her message of love and peace."*

I continued hearing the message that was coming through me. *"You must tell people to put their prejudices, personal beliefs and interest on the side. This song is supposed to be a gift to the world. Therefore, you must donate 100% of the proceeds to help people who are victims of war around the world, see LIGHT through darkness! If anyone understands that, it is you, Aimmee."*

What I experienced that day was magical. In that moment, I felt as if I were in a completely different world. As soon as I came back to myself, I grabbed the phone and called Stephanie. I shared with her my experience and I asked her to come over with a notebook and help me write a song that represents peace through the eyes of that twelve year old little girl. I had no doubt in my mind and heart that Stephanie was meant to share my message with the world through her powerful and gifted voice!

The rest of the story is history. The right people stepped in and volunteered and did everything they could to help us. Nine months later, the "Rise Above" song was born.

Stephanie is one of the many people who was brave enough to allow me to help her see her light. She made the decision to step in and step up to embrace and appreciate her gift. Now, she's helping people see and feel their light through her voice.

* * *

My father once told me, "Aimmee, life is a mystery. It is impossible to know everything. Before we even start to learn what life is all about, we pass away.

The only way we learn about life is from people and loved ones who are willing to share their wisdom with us. We also learn from our own unique life experiences." Every time he shared his wisdom with me, I was inspired.

You may recall what my father shared with me a few days after Robert's death . . .

"Aimmee, look at me. I want you to look straight into my eyes." With love and compassion he continued, "our eyes have three parts, one white, one with color and one black. Do you see what I'm talking about?"

"Yes, I do," I answered. I still wasn't sure why he was telling me this.

"You see the tiny black part of the eye, the innermost circle is called the pupil. We only see through the black part of our eye," he said. "Sometimes we have to go through darkness to see the light."

This is one of many things my father passed on to me which impacted my life in so many different ways.

Since that day, I learned that it is my duty and responsibility to pass on and share all the lessons and insights I picked up along my journey. One thing I truly came to understand is that *giving is living* and I wanted to make sure I gave an opportunity to other souls who will appreciate the power of wisdom.

*   *   *

While I was finishing the last chapter of this book, I felt Robert's spirit close to me. No matter where I went, I sensed his presence as if he were right there. I assumed it was simply because I was so far into the book and all the memories.

As I got to the end of the last chapter, I continued feeling Robert's spirit.

My husband felt that there was something different about how I was behaving. "Why are you sitting on the floor like that?" he would ask.

"Oh nothing, I'm just stretching," I'd reply, as I wiped my tears away so he wouldn't notice.

The next morning, I woke up, made my coffee and meditated for a few moments. Then, I started my usual routine and prepared myself to finish writing the final paragraphs. I sat down at my desk and took a few deep breaths and turned on my laptop and started writing.

I was so excited about sharing my closing thoughts. It didn't take too long before I felt overwhelmed. I pushed the laptop away, got up from my desk and walked toward the living room. Sitting down on the carpet, I began praying for guidance. Within a few moments, I started feeling Robert's spirit. I immediately felt swept back into my past. I was that innocent twelve year old little girl who was still in her pajamas talking to her big brother. It was an unbelievable experience. I felt like I was literally watching a movie in slow motion. Then, I heard Robert say, "I'm so proud of you Aimmee. You didn't become a teacher, you became a healer. The world needs you. Go out there and stand up for the peace you believe in!"

* * *

I hope by now you have discovered the reason why you picked up and read *Tears of Hope* and that what I have shared with you has touched your soul and inspired you to see your life in a different perspective, rise above your challenges and pass your wisdom on to the next generation.

I want you to know that your light and voice matter to the world. I truly know and believe deep in my core, that together, we can make a difference.

It was a pleasure having you on my journey. I hope you join me on my mission of reaching out to people around the world, helping them see *light* through darkness!

With Love and Light,
Aimmee

PICTURES

Aimmee Kodachian

Stephanie Thompson

Stephanie and Aimmee
recording the "Rise Above" song at the studio

Recording the "Rise Above" video at
the CoBiz Coworking, Las Vegas, NV

Eliane Ayele supporting Aimmee's

"Rise above" mission Eliane Ayele and Mitzi Reed
supporting Aimmee's "Rise Above" mission

Two of the dancers for the"Rise Above" video,
Gabrielle Dalton and Trinity Moore

Charmaine Lee instructing the kids
on dancing for the "Rise Above" Song

Cody Herd, Kasandra Robles, Izel Robles, Sydney Lin,
Beata Palo Stricklin. Gabrielle Dalton, Shainna Alipon,
Bella Smith, Kevin Graeser, Nalani Paliotta, Trinity Moore,
Stephanie Thompson and Aimmee Kodachian
(The two little girls in front wearing white
are Aimmee's Granddaughters)

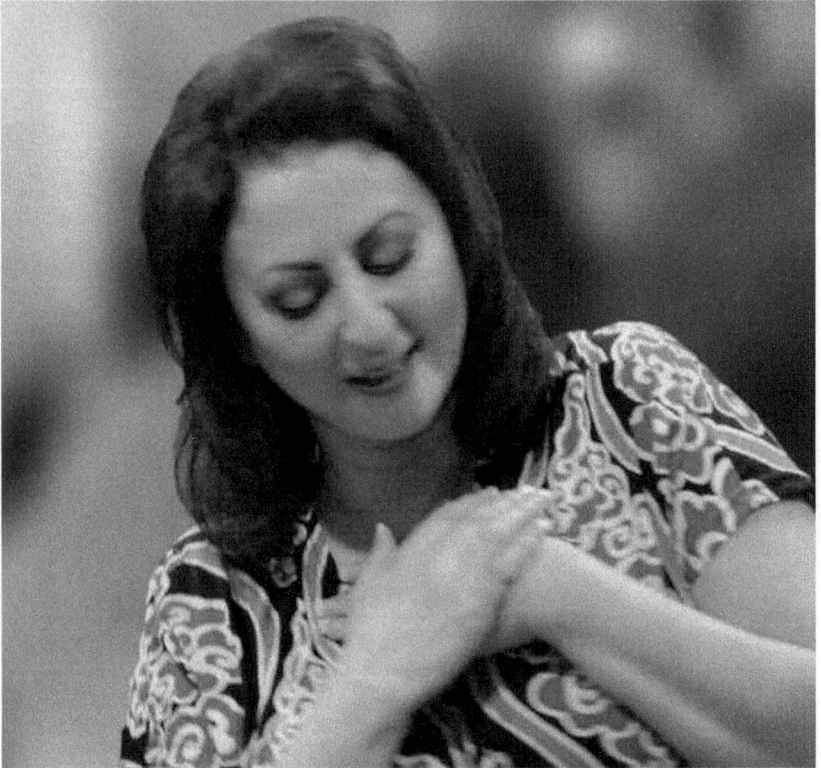

From the bottom of my heart, I would like to thank
Stephanie Thompson for stepping in and helping me with
my mission and to everyone who helped make this possible
and believing in making the world a better place!

To watch the *FREE* "Rise Above" video and see how you
can make a difference in this world, Please visit: **www.
EmpoweringSoulsINT.com**

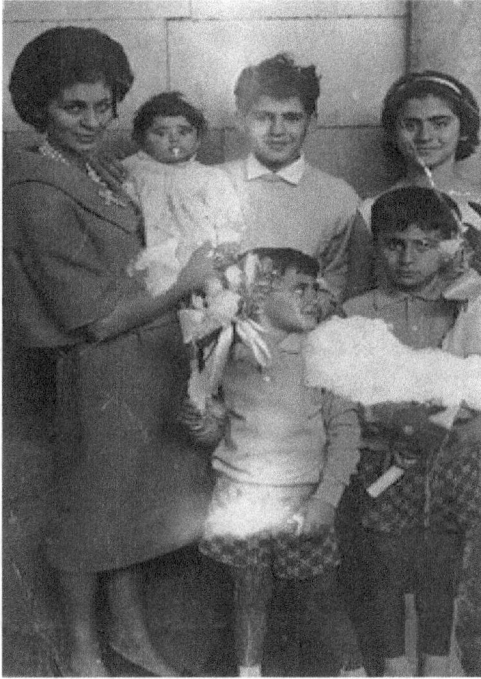

Aimmee around nine months old with her mom,
older brothers and sister

A week before the 1975 Lebanese Civil War

Robert at 20, shortly before the war

Elie at 24

Aimmee's Dad, Bedros "Pierre" Kodachian

Pierre with one of his many inventions "air – purifying"

Aimmee's younger brother Roger during the war

The apartment complex next to where Aimmee lived when
the car bomb that made international news struck. Three
buildings were completely destroyed. This is the setting
where Aimmee escaped death for the 2nd time

Aimmee in her wedding dress exactly 3 days
after her 14th birthday.

Aimmee holding baby Silva, wearing black to honor
her Brother-in-Law, Hagob. The marked building in
the background was destroyed by the car bomb
that made international news

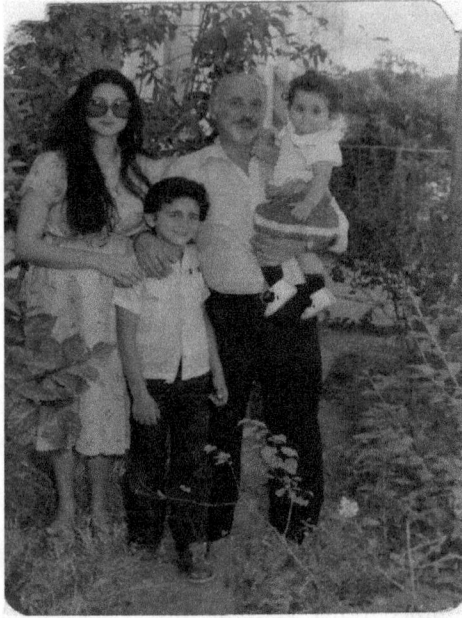

Here is Aimmee pregnant with her second child at 16.
With her dad, Baby Silva and Roger

Aimmee's short modeling career

Roger, Aimmee, Jacqueline, Jacque and their mother
Antoinette in 2003. It was the first time the entire
Kodachian family had been together in more than 2 decades

Aimmee when she met her husband Tom

Aimmee's daughter's college graduation

Aimmee's grandson's graduation

Aimmee and her daughter, Silva, in the United States
smiling after years of determination and persistence

Aimmee's 4 Grandchildren

Aimmee's interview with Mitzi Reed
at the Aspire Women Conference

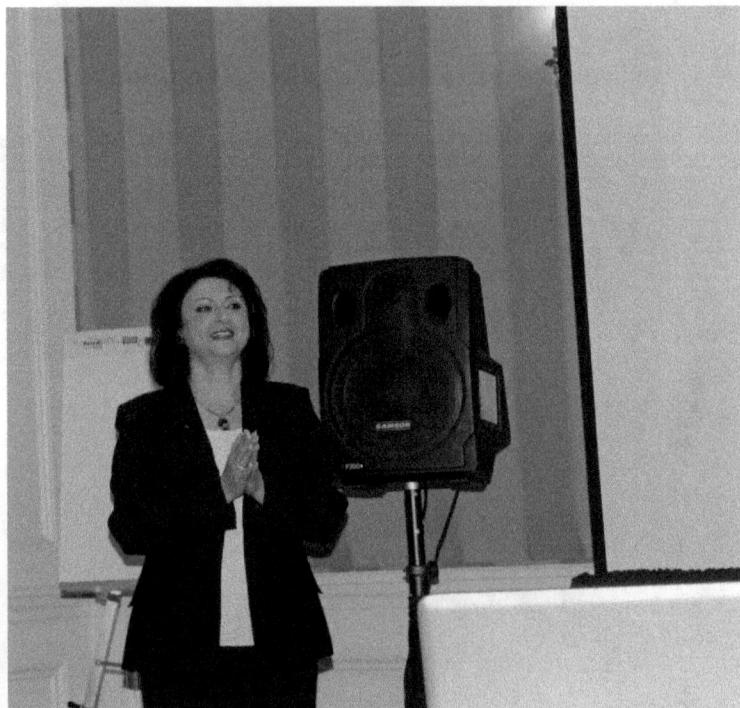

Aimmee speaking at the Beam Institute

Aimmee with Patricia Fripp (an award-winning,
Hall of Fame Speaker, Author and Coach)

Aimmee with Daren LaCroix,
2001 World Champion of Public Speaking

Aimmee at a Barnes and Nobles book signing

Judi Moreo (Internationally known Author, Speaker and Coach) with Aimmee

Aimmee at one of her seminars

Aimmee speaking at one of her events

Aimmee making the final touches on "Tears of Hope"

To learn more about how Aimmee is helping people around the world see *light* through darkness, Please visit:
www.EmpoweringSoulsINT.com

CPSIA information can be obtained
at www.ICGtesting.com
Printed in the USA
FSHW011715100619
58920FS

9 781628 650204